WORLD HISTORY LIBRARY

AFRICA
1 5 0 0 – 1 9 0 0

CONSTANCE JONES

Facts On File
New York

On the cover: A 17th-century bronze plaque with king and musicians, from Benin, Nigeria

Africa: 1500–1900

Copyright © 1993 by Constance Jones

Facts On File, Inc.
460 Park Avenue South
New York NY 10016
USA

Library of Congress Cataloging-in-Publication Data
Jones, Constance, 1961–
    A short history of Africa, 1500–1900 / Constance Jones.
      p. cm. — (World history library)
    Includes bibliographical references and index.
    Summary: Examines the history of Africa from the sixteenth through the nineteenth century, discussing such topics as the different cultures that existed on the continent, the importance of Islam, European colonization, and the slave trade.
    ISBN 0-8160-2774-9 (acid-free paper)
    1. Africa—History—Juvenile literature. [1. Africa—History.]
  I. Title. II. Series.
  DT22.J64 1993
  960'.2—dc20   92-22677

A British CIP catalogue record for this book is available from the British Library.

Facts On File books are available at special discounts when purchased in bulk quantities for businesses, associations, institutions or sales promotions. Please contact our Special Sales Department in New York at 212/683-2244 (dial 800/322-8755).
Text design by Donna Sinisgalli
Jacket design by Amy Gonzalez
Composition by Facts On File, Inc.
Manufacturing by the Maple-Vail Book Manufacturing Group
Printed in the United States of America

10 9 8 7 6 5 4 3 2 1

This book is printed on acid-free paper.

CONTENTS

A PORTRAIT OF AFRICA IN 1500

Africa lies at the center of the earth's cluster of seven continents, yet in 1500 it was all but unknown to outsiders. A land of great topographical and cultural variety where rich kingdoms and empires had flourished for thousands of years, Africa had little contact with the rest of the world at the beginning of the 16th century. Arab traders scattered across North Africa, the Sahara and the east coast, Turkish soldiers ruling Egypt and a small number of Portuguese merchants operating from coastal bases in western and eastern Africa represented the few foreigners with firsthand knowledge of the continent in 1500.

It had not always been so. In ancient times Phoenicians, Greeks and Romans had traded with and sometimes ruled the inhabitants of northern Africa, and only a few hundred years had passed since that region had been part of the Muslim empire of the Arabs. Along the east coast, Arab and Indian merchants occasionally passed through trading towns. Only in southern and central Africa, isolated from the rest of the continent by the double barrier of the Sahara desert and the thick equatorial rain forest, did the indigenous cultures develop entirely free from external influence. By 1500, though, few of the early visitors remained in northern Africa. Africans were building on their own rich artistic, political, economic and social traditions, continuing a long and proud history. But a new and troubled era dawned for Africa when a new wave of Europeans started to arrive in the years leading up to 1500.

AN ABUNDANT LAND

The African story unfolds on a vast continent that sits astride the equator. Second in size only to Asia, Africa is about as wide as it is long and encompasses about 11.7 million square miles (30.3 million square kilometers) of land. Directly to the north, across the Mediterranean Sea, lies Europe. Asia lies to the northeast, across the narrow expanse of the Red Sea. The Indian Ocean separates Africa's east coast from Australia and its southern tip from Antarctica. Across the Atlantic Ocean to the west are North and South America. At its extremes, Africa reaches almost as far north as Washington, D.C. and San Francisco, California; as far south as Buenos Aires, Argentina; almost as far west as Reykjavik, Iceland; and as far east as Tehran, Iran.

Africa is essentially a large plateau that rises abruptly from the sea. Its steeply sloped coastline boasts few of the broad plains typically found along the coasts of other continents. This fact, combined with the almost complete lack of natural harbors, long made Africa forbidding to foreign sailors. Beyond the coastal areas, most of the continent's terrain consists of flatlands and low hills, except for a few minor mountain ranges, isolated volcanoes and the rugged Ethiopian Highlands. Several significant islands, such as Madagascar, and island groups, such as the Canary Islands, lie off its coasts. On the mainland, Africa's major topographical features are the Sahara, a desert that occupies most of the northern third of the landmass, and the lakes of the eastern region, including Lake Victoria and Lake Tanganyika. Its longest river is the mighty Nile (the longest river in the world), followed by the Congo, the Niger and the Zambezi.

Because the equator divides the continent almost exactly in half, Africa enjoys a uniformly warm climate. Rainfall varies widely, though, producing diverse environments for plants, animals and people. The area surrounding the equator, for instance, receives at least 60 to 80 inches (150 to 200 centimeters) of rain annually and is covered by lush tropical rain forest. All kinds of birds, reptiles, insects and mammals—including apes, gorillas and hippopotamuses—abound in this jungle. By contrast, the Sahara, along with the Kalahari Desert of southwestern Africa, receives only a few inches of rainfall each year and supports little vegetation or animal life. A few oases and the verdant Nile River valley do, however, offer some relief to camels and people in the Sahara.

Two other types of habitat complete the African landscape. Immediately to the north and south of the rain-forest region is a drier zone of wooded savannah, tropical grassland dotted with trees and shrubs. There elephants, rhinoceroses, giraffes, leopards and hoofed animals predominate. Bordering the Kalahari on the east and the Sahara on the south is steppe, arid grassland where few trees grow. Antelopes, zebras and other hoofed animals live in the steppe, along with predators such as lions, cheetahs and hyenas. Steppe and woodland mix on the continent's southern tip and on its Mediterranean coast, where relatively dense human population wiped out most native wildlife by 1500.

THE CRADLE OF CIVILIZATION

Although Portuguese adventurers arriving in Africa in the 15th century may have viewed the territory as the "Dark Continent," a savage, untamed wilderness, Africa in fact had a longer history than either Europe or Asia, and housed civilizations that at times had been far more advanced than any others on earth. With such a varied and hospitable climate (the Sahara did not become a desert until 3000 to 2000 B.C.), it is not surprising that Africa was the spot where the first human beings lived. What many scientists believe to be the oldest known hominid (prehuman) fossil on earth was discovered in modern Ethiopia. Dubbed "Lucy" by scientists, the remains are thought to date back 3.5 million years. Later fossils and artifacts found in eastern Africa trace the physical evolution of the region's hominids and their earliest use of tools and fire.

At some point many thousands of years ago, hominids began spreading from their East African home throughout the continent as well as to southern Asia and Europe. Evolution continued wherever they went, but fossil records show that the earliest identifiable *Homo sapiens*—humans—appeared in East Africa around 20,000 B.C. First as hunter-gatherers and later as farmers and herders, Africans developed simple societies that number among the world's earliest. South of the Sahara, where tropical conditions rendered the rudimentary agricultural knowledge of North Africa useless, Africans had to devise unique farming methods for crops unknown elsewhere. This added challenge delayed the development of complex political, economic and cultural systems in sub-Saharan Africa, but to the north one of the world's great civilizations—and arguably the first—rose in the 4th millennium B.C.

Long before they traveled to Africa, Europeans had heard of the Great Pyramids along the Nile, the majestic remains of the faded civilization of Egypt. The ancestors of the Egyptians started cultivating grain on the floodplains of the Nile River valley between 5000 and 4000 B.C. They invented the first calendar, which marks the earliest recorded date in human history as 4241 B.C. Harnessing the floodwaters of the Nile to irrigate their crops required the cooperation of large numbers of people in an organized enterprise, so governments arose to supervise the annual effort. In 3110 B.C. two such kingdoms united under Menes, the first pharaoh, launching the first of many Egyptian dynasties.

By the time the Egyptians built the Great Pyramids, in the 26th century B.C., they had originated systems of writing, arithmetic, geometry, astronomy and surveying as well as the first 365-day calendar. A complex government bureaucracy and religion lent order to their lives, while sophisticated arts and architecture lent it beauty. The wealthy empire grew and shrank under successive dynasties, at times extending from the northeast corner of Africa far into Asia. The golden age of Egypt lasted until the 12th century B.C., after which the Egyptians lived more humbly, sometimes ruled by others.

Even as Egypt's glory dimmed, the kingdom of Kush, also known as Nubia, rose to the south. The people living along the upper Nile had traded with the Egyptians for hundreds of years and raised grains and cattle to feed themselves. Ruled by Egyptians from about 1500 B.C., Kushites established an independent nation by 1000 B.C. The Egyptianized Kushites gradually developed their own language and script and gained a reputation as the region's best ironworkers. Meroe, an ancient Kushite city on the upper Nile, reflects Egyptian influence

Egypt was one of the first great African empires. This scene of sowing, hoeing and ploughing is on the walls of the tomb of Nakhti at Sheikh Abd-el-Kurnah. Nakhti was in the service of the Temple of Ammon at Thebes during the 18th dynasty, late 2nd century B.C. (Picture Collection, The Branch Libraries, The New York Public Library)

in some of its architecture. The Kushites grew wealthy trading gold, ivory, animal hides and aromatic oils for goods offered by the inhabitants of northern Africa, prospering until about A.D. 300.

Along the Mediterranean coast, meanwhile, three major foreign powers established significant if temporary presences. The Phoenicians, seafaring traders from the region now known as Lebanon, built the city of Carthage on the site of present-day Tunis. From about 810 B.C. Carthage controlled east–west traffic in the Mediterranean and became a powerful trading center. The Carthaginians conquered the entire North African coast from modern Tripoli to Tangier and even laid claim to most of eastern Spain.

After arriving on the eastern Mediterranean coast between Carthage and Egypt, the ancient Greeks founded the African city of Cyrene and the colony of Cyrenaica in the 7th century B.C. They tried but failed to take Carthage, though they soon exerted a strong influence on Egypt. From about 525 B.C. to about 330 B.C. the Greek colonies and Egypt fell under Persian (Iranian) control, but when the Greek leader Alexander the Great . later conquered Persia, Cyrenaica and Egypt were again ruled by the Greeks. Alexander installed Ptolemy as the king of Egypt, and until the 1st century A.D. Greece and Egypt exchanged the world's most advanced scientific, political, economic and artistic knowledge.

All of North Africa eventually fell to the Romans: Carthage by 150 B.C., Egypt by 30 B.C. and Cyrenaica by A.D. 42. The Romans imported Christianity to the region and named their territory there *Africa*, a name the world soon applied to the entire continent. Although the Romans ruled North Africa for hundreds of years, in other parts of the continent Africans were busy building their own societies free of outside interference. In West Africa, merchant cultures arose to take advantage of trade routes plied by Berber nomads across the western Sahara. The pastoral peoples of eastern and southern Africa, meanwhile, farmed grains, vegetables and cattle.

Just south of Kush, as that empire declined about A.D. 300, the kingdom of Aksum took form. Located on the northern edge of the Ethiopian Highlands, Aksum enjoyed an ideal position for trade with its northern neighbors, other East Africans and even India. Trading in spices, natural gums and tortoiseshell, the Aksumites flourished until warfare in North Africa disrupted commerce about A.D. 700. The Aksumites then migrated south and settled in the territory that would become Ethiopia, a Christian kingdom that eventually captured the imagination of 15th- and 16th-century Europeans.

ARAB INFLUENCE IN THE GREAT AGE OF ISLAM

The Africans who first met Portuguese mariners landing on their shores were probably Muslims, practitioners of Islam, a religion that originated in the Arab lands of the Middle East. Far more than the Phoenicians, Greeks or Romans ever did, Arab Muslims had a profound effect on the culture of Africa north of the equatorial rain forests. Inspired by the desire to convert all the world to Islam, Arab warriors first invaded Africa in A.D. 639. By A.D. 708 the Arabs expelled the Romans and ruled all of Africa north of the Sahara. Several centuries of Islamic influence all but obliterated Christianity and other religions there and changed the face of North African society.

As Arabs and Africans mixed genetically and culturally, they formed a new Muslim people known to Europeans as the Moors. The Moors conquered Spain in the 8th century and for hundreds of years led the world in government, the arts, science, mathematics, agriculture, architecture and virtually every other field. Their influence spread to Iraq, Persia (Iran), Syria and France as well as to West Africa. The Sahara desert prevented the Moors from invading the rest of the continent, but Islam spread peacefully via trade routes. Tent-dwelling nomads from the Arabian deserts migrated to the northern edges of the Sahara, where they blended with the indigenous Berber nomads. These nomads traveled the desert for the purposes of trade and brought Islam with them wherever they went.

Many non-Moorish African leaders saw the economic and political advantages of converting to Islam: They could benefit from trade with the Moors, while Islamic principles of equality and brotherhood would help them rule large groups of diverse people under a single set of laws. Few ordinary non-Moorish Africans converted, but by the 14th century many of their leaders north of the equator called themselves Muslims.

Along with coherent governmental systems that allowed for the growth of more extensive kingdoms, Islam brought education and literacy to large segments of the North African upper classes. African culture flourished while Europe sank into the violent and oppressive era known as the Dark Ages. The region south of the equator was little affected by the advent of Islam and the inhabitants of Ethiopia resisted its pull, but Muslim empires ruled by people of mixed Arab and African blood encompassed large tracts of northern Africa. The first of these, the Fatimid empire, reached its greatest extent in the late 10th century. By the 12th century the Almoravid empire dominated, followed in the 13th century by the Almohad empire. The Moors who controlled these territories were so powerful that some even ruled the Arab lands of the Middle East.

Direct Arab influence in Africa waned by 1300, when the Arab empire came under attack from aggressors such as the Turks, and from Spaniards and Portuguese seeking to free themselves from outside control. Nonetheless, the Moors still occupied much of Spain when the Portuguese first arrived in Africa; they would not be ejected completely until 1492.

AFRICA'S MAJOR CULTURES IN 1500

The Africa approached by Portuguese sailors in the 15th century was a land of immense cultural variety. Divided into five states that stood side by side along the northern coast, the North Africans remained an Islamic people. Their economy was based on trade with Italians and Arabs via the Mediterranean Sea. The Egyptians to the east were ruled by Turkish soldiers known as Mamluks, who had originally been imported as slaves to expand the military under the Fatimid dynasty. Berber nomad tribes such as the Tuareg controlled the Sahara; they were also Muslim.

In the strip of savannah and steppe, known as the Sudan, that divides the Sahara desert to the north from the jungle to the south, numerous societies thrived. There the empire of Songhai was in the process of taking control of the Niger River from the kingdom of Mali. Songhai was the third empire to rise in the rich gold-mining region of the western Sudan. The first major power to use the wealth of the region to advantage had been the ancient kingdom of Ghana, which originated in the last few centuries B.C. and lasted until the late 12th century A.D. It was overshadowed when a group of Malinke chiefdoms allied to tap new sources of gold in the region, forming the state of Mali. Mali succeeded Ghana as the western Sudan's dominant power and endured until the 15th century, when Songhai assumed control. Europeans ventured to Africa in part because of the legendary wealth of these empires.

To the south, forest peoples such as the Yoruba and the Ife had started to produce sculpture, masks and other objects of exceptional beauty as well as joyful and complex percussion-based music. The foundations of the Hausa city-states, which would begin their rise to power in the 16th century, were firmly in place in the area now known as Nigeria. Eastward, in the central Sudan, the kingdom of Kanem-Borno controlled the area around Lake Chad. Exporting ivory, ostrich feathers and slaves, Kanem based its wealth on trade with Egypt and other North African countries across the central Sahara.

To the east of the Sudan, near the mouth of the Red Sea, the kingdom of Ethiopia struggled to protect its territory. Built on the ashes of extinct Aksum, Ethiopia cultivated grain, herded cattle and traded with its Egyptian and Arab neighbors. Territorial and religious disputes with Muslims plagued the kingdom from the 10th century onward, and in the 15th century Ethiopia was at war almost constantly. The conflict placed a severe strain on the Ethiopian people and their economy, but a strong cultural identity kept the kingdom alive. The name *Ethiopia* combines the Greek words *ethios*, meaning "black," and *ops*, meaning "face." The ancient Greeks applied the label to all people darker than themselves, so for many centuries Europeans referred to all Africans, Asians and Indians as Ethiopians. In more recent centuries Europeans narrowed their use of the term to describe the inhabitants of the ancient outpost of Christianity in Muslim- and pantheist-dominated Africa. They hoped some day to find Ethiopia and establish ties with its people in order to gain a foothold in Africa for a campaign against the Muslim "infidels."

To the south of Ethiopia, along Africa's eastern coast, a string of about 40 independent city-states engaged in maritime trade. These small principalities, each no larger than a single town, were inhabited by Swahili-speaking people who had Arab as well as African blood. They obtained ivory, furs and gold from tribes living in the continent's interior and traded these goods with Arab, Indian and Indonesian merchants who arrived by sea. Although the Swahili city-states competed fiercely for trade, they rarely fought with each other. Nor did they attempt to conquer their neighbors in the interior, peoples who lived largely as farmers and hunters.

At the time the first Portuguese explored the African coast, central and southern Africa was home to dozens of societies that anthropologists have described as "later Iron Age" states. Largely isolated from contact with outsiders other than those much like themselves, these peoples worked to improve their agricultural, cattle herding and fishing techniques and to develop better ways of manufacturing pottery and metal objects. They traded among themselves and, in the eastern regions, with the Swahili merchants of the coast. Ruled by chiefs or kings, these people included the Kongo and the Ndongo along the central west coast, the Luba and the Lunda of the central interior and the Torwa and Mutapa farther to the east. Africa's southernmost inhabitants at the turn of the 16th century included the Tswana, the Sotho, the Khoikhoi and the San.

THE ARRIVAL OF THE PORTUGUESE

Attracted by the potential wealth to be found in Africa—most notably in the form of gold, ivory and slaves—Europeans planned their arrival long before they could carry it out. They hoped to chart the continent's coastline and find out if they could reach the rich trade of India and Asia by sailing around it. Technological advances during the Moorish occupation of the 8th to 15th centuries eventually gave Spain and Portugal the naval capabilities they needed to conduct such a venture. For the first time, they built ships that could travel long distances on the high seas, powered by sail and strong enough to withstand pounding surf. In Portugal, the successful battle to force the Moors out had produced a strong monarchy capable of commanding an ambitious exploration. The fight had also trained the Portuguese military for large-scale operations.

In addition to establishing trading bases, the Portuguese, like other Christian Europeans, hoped to crush Islam. The first Portuguese expedition to Africa, led by Prince Henry, affirmed both these goals by capturing the Moroccan town of Ceuta in 1415. Henry set up his African headquarters there, from which he planned to supervise the exploration of the West African coast. The prince's activities over the next 45 years earned him the nickname "Henry the Navigator." Under his direction, the Portuguese navy moved steadily down the coast. They settled Madeira in 1419 and the Azores in 1439. Upon reaching Cape Verde in 1444, they colonized the Cape Verde Islands to use as a trading base.

Along the way, the sailors came upon rich coastal fishing banks from which their country could profit. The western coastland along the

Sahara, however, offered little to attract their attention. They pressed on, reaching the coast of present-day Sierra Leone in 1460, the year Henry died. Hired explorers continued the journey and crossed the equator in 1471. Once past the equator, the Portuguese found what they had been looking for: gold. Along the Gold Coast of West Africa, they came upon wealthy gold-trading empires and sent news of their find to their king. Seeking to protect their discovery from competitors, the Portuguese court secured orders from the pope (at that time the highest authority in the Christian world) granting Portugal possession of all the territory it "discovered." Neither the pope nor the Portuguese seemed to consider the fact that African states had occupied the area for thousands of years.

The explorers continued, passing the mouth of the Congo River in 1483 and finally rounding the southern tip of Africa in 1488. Meanwhile, aware of the established navigating routes of traders along the eastern coast, the Portuguese decided to explore the shoreline following the traditional direction of travel, north to south. They set sail on the Indian Ocean in 1487 and reached Ethiopia in 1490. There Pero de Covilha, a Portuguese representative, met with Ethiopian rulers to inaugurate diplomatic relations. Seven years later Vasco de Gama completed the Portuguese exploration of the African coastline, sailing down the western coast, around the Cape of Good Hope, up the eastern coast and across the Indian Ocean to India. This journey not only charted the continent's limits but marked a direct water route between Portugal and India, which at the time was the most desirable destination for European traders.

By 1500, with the completion of the initial Portuguese exploration, Europe had taken the first steps toward exploiting the resources of Africa. Largely unknown to Europeans, Africa supported numerous civilizations with complex cultures, rich traditions and long histories. In the four centuries to come these two contrasting societies would collide, sometimes benefiting from the contact but more often suffering profound damage. Africans would fight, with greater or lesser success, to preserve their identity and their independence in the face of the European invasion. In the end, the battle would change the course of world history.

THE CULTURES
OF NORTH
AFRICA AND
THE SAHARA

Set apart from the rest of Africa geographically, racially and culturally, North Africa has a history quite different from that of the continent south of the Sahara desert. Its people are largely Caucasian rather than Negroid, and they first came into contact with the outside world much earlier, via trade with Europeans across the Mediterranean and with Arabs across the Red Sea. North Africa's ties to the Arab world were particularly strong due to the influence of Islam, which conquering Arab invaders introduced to the region in the 7th century. Islam quickly took root and spread throughout the territory, bringing with it distinctive political, social and cultural ideas. As Arabs settled in the coastal areas and nomadic tribes migrated from Arabia to the Sahara, they intermarried with the local peoples. By 1500 North Africa was thoroughly Muslim and strongly Arabic, right down to its inhabitants' language, dress and diet.

Still, North Africa was part of the African continent. Trade routes across the Sahara linked it with societies in West Africa, the Sudan and

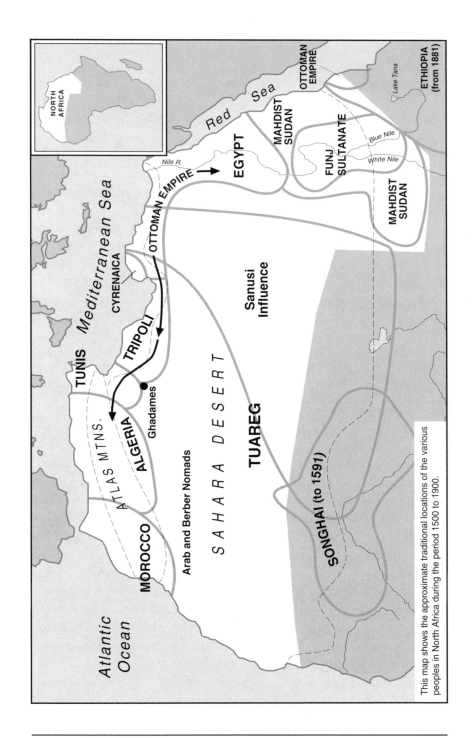

This map shows the approximate traditional locations of the various peoples in North Africa during the period 1500 to 1900.

Ethiopia. Indeed, trade with sub-Saharan peoples was vital to the prosperity of North Africans. Manufactured items, such as leather and metal goods, and raw materials, such as gold and ivory, traveled north by caravan for sale to wealthy local Muslims and for export to Europe and the Middle East. In exchange, North African merchants sent imported European goods, such as glass and armaments, and locally produced items, such as textiles and salt, to the south. Most profitable, however, was the trade in slaves captured in the Sudan and in the equatorial rain forest and brought north for sale to Arab, Indian and European buyers.

For centuries, North Africa served as a sort of international cultural meeting place where local Africans successfully absorbed foreign influences into their society and, in turn, made their mark on outsiders. The area enjoyed periods of great prosperity as well as episodes of turmoil, developing a rich culture that blended elements of African, Arabic and European civilization. The societies of North Africa long managed to preserve their autonomy, even as they encountered foreign colonizers intent on claiming the region's wealth for themselves. But over the course of the 19th century, most of North Africa succumbed to the superior military might of the Europeans and joined the rest of the continent in colonial bondage.

AN ISLAMIC CULTURE

North Africa consists of two basic regions: the coastal area, a strip of land 100 to 400 miles (161 to 645 kilometers) wide that hugs the Mediterranean Sea and the Atlantic Ocean; and the Sahara desert, a swath of sand 1,000 miles (1,610 kilometers) wide that cuts across the entire upper continent. Blessed with a temperate Mediterranean climate and fertile though dry soil, the coastal area has always been home to most of North Africa's population. The Sahara, meanwhile, supports only a few nomadic clans that travel from camp to camp in small groups. The city dwellers of Algiers, the peasant farmers of the Nile River valley and the Berber nomads of the Sahara live vastly different lives, but they long have been united by Islam. Since its arrival in the 7th century, Islam has been the single most important component of North African culture.

Military conquest by Arab invaders as well as trade and intermarriage between Arabs and Africans allowed Islam to spread over all

North Africa during medieval times (7th through 15th centuries). During the centuries from 1500 to 1900, Islamic customs and beliefs permeated North African society and determined the patterns of life there. Because education was highly valued, literacy was widespread and the arts and sciences flourished. Technological and administrative advances improved agriculture in the coastal areas and on the flood-plains of the Nile. Relative peace brought prosperity, as merchants and traders took advantage of cultural and political ties with fellow Muslims. The governing elite in each country developed an organized bureaucracy to tax the population and provide public services, but mostly to put together a strong military. Internal power struggles and interference from foreigners sometimes sparked wars, and the urban and farming populations frequently had to defend themselves against marauding nomads, but the most serious threat ultimately faced by North Africa came from Europe.

EGYPT—MAMLUKS, PASHAS AND MAHDISTS

In 1500 Egypt, the ancient land of the pharaohs, reflected little of the glory it had once known. Its 4 or 5 million people suffered the harsh rule of the Mamluks, a cadre of military officers who taxed the peasantry heavily and forced young Egyptian men into military service. The Mamluks were descended from slave warriors imported from Turkey by the Arabs who ruled Egypt from the 7th to the 13th century. After a period of service the Mamluks were granted freedom, land and the right to tax the Egyptians who lived on that land. They evolved into a sort of local nobility and in 1250 murdered the Arab sultan, claiming the sole right to rule Egypt. Their greed and corruption, along with a series of natural disasters, plunged the country into famine during the 1400s. Meanwhile, competition from Portuguese traders, who had arrived on the Indian Ocean in the 1490s, sharply reduced Egypt's mercantile revenues.

The weakened country made easy prey for ambitious foreigners, especially since the Mamluks failed to update their military with the recently introduced firearms used throughout Europe and the Middle East. Seeing an opportunity to expand their empire, the Ottomans of Turkey—a country that straddles Europe and Asia—invaded Egypt in 1517. They easily defeated the disorganized and ill-equipped Mamluks

---

ISLAM

In the Arabic language, the word *Islam* means "universal submission." The prophet Muhammad, born in Mecca on the Arabian peninsula in about A.D. 570, made Islam the name of the religion he founded. This religion required the universal submission of all the world's people to a single god, Allah. Christians and Jews had adopted the principle of monotheism—belief in a single god—centuries before Muhammad appeared, but the Arab prophet used the powerful concept to build Islam into a complex social and political system as well as a religion. True believers in the teachings of Muhammad, those who submit themselves to the will of Allah, are called Muslims; their sacred text is the Koran. In that text are recorded the revelations of the prophet, including the central tenet that "There is no god but Allah: Muhammad is the messenger of Allah."

The Koran establishes Friday as the sabbath and ordains that believers should pray to Allah at five specific times each day of the week. Devout Muslims must also donate a tenth of their income to help the needy and to advance Islam, and they must fast between dawn and sundown during the holy month of Ram-

and pushed southward up the Nile, expanding Egyptian territory to include the northern reaches of old Nubia. This campaign allowed the Ottomans to secure control of a long stretch of the lower Nile and much of the Red Sea coast. In doing so, they prevented the Portuguese from further eroding Egypt's trade with India. The Red Sea was vital to the Egyptian economy, for Egypt did a booming import-export business in Asian goods sent on to Europe.

The Ottomans might have taken their conquest farther south were it not for the presence of the Funj Sultanate along the middle Nile. This empire arose early in the 16th century, when the area's people, known as the Funj, converted to Islam. Traditionally keepers of cattle and horses, the Funj had long lived in scattered groups headed by local chieftains. Conversion to Islam allowed a few leaders to unite the Funj adan (the ninth month of the Islamic calendar, which is a lunar calendar and thus has 11 fewer days than the solar calendar used in the West). A pilgrimage to Mecca completes the religious requirements of a Muslim life. Because Allah is considered the only true god, idolatry is prohibited and creating images of Allah, of human beings or of animals is forbidden. Devotion to Allah also demands that Muslims forsake worldly pleasures and lead a moderate life, so some sects ban alcohol and other stimulants and require women to wear modest clothing that covers their hair, their face or their entire body.

While Islam puts women in a position of subordination to men, the creed emphasizes the brotherhood and equality of all Muslim men. Regardless of family, tribal or national affiliation, every Muslim male who submits to the will of Allah is believed to be equal in God's eyes. Devotion to Allah supercedes all other loyalties; therefore, Islam has the potential to unite warring groups and draw together diverse populations under a single banner. This doctrine was one of the key aspects of Islam in precolonial North Africa, for it helped local rulers form alliances and gain control of larger territories. North Africa's conversion to Islam lent the region a degree of cultural unity and a shared system of beliefs.

in an empire centered on the spot where the Nile River branches into the White Nile and the Blue Nile. The local rulers retained their authority, but the new Funji sultan taxed the people in order to raise an army that could protect the entire territory. Under the sultan's watchful eye, the Funji military became a well-trained force.

Although the Ottomans were rebuffed by the Funji Sultanate, they made Egypt a province of the Turkish empire and temporarily removed the Mamluks from power. Turkey's sultan appointed governors, called pashas, to rule the territory, and for a few years conditions improved for ordinary Egyptians. By the 17th century, however, the Mamluks regained control of the government as appointees of a new sultan. Based a thousand miles away in Constantinople, the Ottomans had little influence over the internal operations of Egypt. Corruption returned along with oppressive taxation as the Mamluks focused on filling their personal treasuries. The influx of tax revenue made Cairo one of the most dazzlingly luxurious cities in the Muslim world, but official neglect of rural conditions led to a decline in agriculture. Nomadic peoples in search of grazing land for their livestock encroached on irrigated farmland. Overgrazing and insufficient maintenance of irrigation systems caused fertile fields and orchards to become deserts once more.

During the 18th century Britain and France engaged in a fierce struggle for control of trade routes to India. Egypt, a strategically located center of commerce with India, became a focus of this struggle. Napoleon Bonaparte, the French general who would become emperor in 1804, knew the Ottomans had only a weak grip on the country. In 1798 he launched an attack and crushed Ottoman rule. But the British would not let Napoleon take Egypt without a fight, and in 1801 the British navy helped the Ottoman sultan force the French out. The conflict left the local Egyptian government in shambles, and several years of political instability ensued. One military officer saw an opportunity in the chaos and began his climb to power.

Muhammad Ali, born in the Ottoman province of Albania, went to Egypt leading Albanian troops who helped expel the French. Once in Egypt, Ali set about achieving his goal of becoming pasha and making that post a hereditary title of his family. His skill as a military leader made him the most powerful man in Egypt by 1805. Recognizing Ali's popularity, the Ottoman sultan named him pasha in 1806. Muhammad Ali's political techniques were a blend of farsightedness and brutality. He established a salaried civil service to replace the corrupt system of administration conducted by appointed officials under previous pashas. He reformed agriculture, introducing new crops such as sugar and cotton, extending irrigation and establishing a profitable export trade. He encouraged Muslims throughout North Africa to make pilgrimages to Mecca, for travelers passing through Egypt spent money along the way. Ali also revived the profitable Red Sea trade in gold, coffee, slaves and civet musk, out of the port of Jidda. That port became an important stopover for British merchants and officials on their way to and from their colony of India.

All these activities helped Egypt to advance into the modern era, but not without cost. The increased revenues flowing into the hands of

Egyptians were heavily taxed so Ali could pay for a large army that kept growing. Equipped with the latest European armaments and trained in European strategy, the Egyptian army was formidable. Backed by this force, Ali murdered hundreds of his Mamluk opponents and forced peasants into military service. He suppressed the rebellion of the Wahhabis, a group of fanatical Muslim nomads who lived in the desert, in a series of bloody encounters. But his successes only made Ali hungrier for more wealth and power, and increasingly fearful that someone might take them from him.

Ali invaded the Funj Sultanate in 1820 and crushed the local leaders the next year. Egypt then raided the Sudan for ivory and slaves, generating even more revenue with which to support its army. The Ottoman sultan called on Ali to assist in putting down rebels in Greece, but British and French forces destroyed the Egyptian navy and Greece gained its independence from Turkey. Despite the defeat, the sultan proclaimed that Ali's descendants would be the hereditary pashas of Egypt. But Ali, loyal only to himself, briefly took Syria and Palestine from Turkey in 1831.

Ali's grandson Ismail became pasha of Egypt in 1864 and continued the effort to expand and modernize the nation. Under his rule, the Suez Canal was completed in 1869 and a network of railroads and telegraph lines went up. These projects, along with ambitious military efforts to extend Egypt's borders, put the country deeply in debt to various European nations. In 1881, when a new threat arose to the south, Egypt was too weak to suppress it. Muhammad Admad, an Islamic fundamentalist living in the Sudan, declared himself the Mahdi (Guided One), a savior who would restore the purity of Islam. Rapidly gaining support from local people who resented the incursion of European-influenced Egyptians, Admad soon had followers throughout a region that reached beyond the old Funj Sultanate. The Mahdists pushed the Egyptians out of the area in 1885 and established the Mahdist Sudan, a state based on the teachings of the Koran. The Mahdist victory over Egypt signaled the end of Egyptian power.

AL-MAGHRIB: TRIPOLI, TUNIS AND ALGERIA

The Arabs who ruled North Africa until the 13th century named the stretch of land between Egypt and Spain al-Maghrib, or "the West."

Encompassing present-day Libya, Tunisia, Algeria and Morocco, most of al-Maghrib (excluding Morocco) was part of the Ottoman Empire in 1500. Turkey's control over the area was minimal, however; beyond paying taxes to the sultan, the nations of al-Maghrib operated almost independent of faraway Constantinople. Although officially accountable to the Turkish ruler, the governments of the three territories—Tripoli, Tunis and Algeria—functioned according to local customs and imperatives. Throughout the region, Ottoman influence did not extend far beyond the larger towns, and the desert nomads remained unaffected by the Turkish presence.

The Africans of al-Maghrib traded freely with other African peoples via trans-Saharan caravan routes and with Europeans via the Mediterranean Sea. Tripoli maintained an especially active mercantile relationship with the sub-Saharan kingdom of Borno and the Hausa city-states, importing such items as leatherwork and kola nuts for sale to the Middle East. Tunis produced wheat in abundance and was famed for its wealth of fruits, textiles, leather goods and metal wares. Algeria, meanwhile, exported grain and olive oil, much of it to France. As elsewhere in Africa, the biggest trade item in al-Maghrib was slaves, exported from West Africa, transported across the Sahara and shipped to Europe and the Middle East from Mediterranean ports. Many of the goods flowing across the desert in either direction passed through an oasis called Ghadames, which stood where the borders of modern Libya, Tunisia and Algeria meet. There entrepreneurs purchased goods from traders arriving from the north and south, then sold them to merchants headed in the opposite direction. Few traders traveled the entire distance from the western Sudan to the Mediterranean coast; instead Ghadames was their destination.

Algiers, Tunis and Tripoli, the major port cities of al-Maghrib, bustled day and night as ships arrived from and departed for Europe and the Middle East. They were also headquarters for the Turkish corsairs (pirates) who engaged in maritime trade, preyed on European merchant vessels and defended Ottoman territory against attack. During the 15th and 16th centuries, when Portuguese and Spanish ships attacked and seized various ports along the North African coast, the Turkish corsairs counterattacked and often took the towns back. Major and minor ports changed hands several times until the 17th century, when the corsairs gained firm control of the entire North African coast. For about a century the corsairs ruled much of the Mediterranean from Algiers, raiding foreign trading ships with impunity. In the 1700s, however, the rise of strong European navies all but ended Turkish corsairing.

Despite their contact with Europe and Turkey, the countries of al-Maghrib were more closely linked—culturally and politically—to the Arab world than to Europe or the Ottoman Empire. The merchants and administrators of the cities, who managed the political and economic life of each nation, were Muslims. They turned to Islam as a unifying and guiding force both within their borders and in relations with neighboring Muslim nations. Marabouts (holy men) and tariquas (religious brotherhoods) played a central role in the political life of the region, determining loyalties and distributing power.

In Tripoli, the pasha appointed by the Ottoman sultan was always a local Muslim and fulfilled his duties according to local custom and Islamic law. The sultan proclaimed that office the hereditary right of the Karamanlis, a local family, in 1714. Between 1795 and 1830, Pasha Yusuf Karamanli used his army to expand the territory under his control, forcing marauding nomads out of the countryside and into the desert. He also entered into treaties with the kingdoms of Borno and Sokoto to the south and set up a trade pipeline that brought 10,000 slaves across the desert annually. Karamanli cultivated friendly relations with Britain, perhaps hoping to enlist British support for a rebellion against Turkey. When he died, Turkey decided to establish tighter control over Tripoli before a new Karamanli could gain power. The Ottomans deposed the Karamanlis in 1836.

Tunis was governed by a military elite descended from Turkish army officers who had married into local families. In Tunis the supreme commander of the military, known as the dey, ruled before 1710. He generally left the daily operations of the country to his second-in-command, the bey. Under a series of corrupt deys in the early 18th century, the bey became increasingly powerful. Finally the position of dey was abolished and the bey was made hereditary leader of Tunis. One of the bey's primary duties was to protect the rural population from attacks by nomadic Berber clans. Thus protected, the country thrived throughout the 18th century. Prosperity allowed Tunis to pursue political reform, even though it remained part of the Ottoman Empire. The nation outlawed piracy in 1819, banned slavery in the 1840s and established a constitutional government in 1857 to 1861. Independence, however, lay years away.

In Algeria, a military leadership similar to that of Tunis ruled the nation under the Ottomans. There the leaders, known as deys, gained office by election. The activities of the corsairs brought wealth to the city of Algiers, which became one of North Africa's loveliest. Trade and agriculture made Algeria a prosperous country in which literacy was widespread. All that marred the peace were periodic raids by Berber nomads and occasional attacks from the independent kingdom of Morocco, which lay to the east. Algeria established strong trading links with France in the 18th century and provisioned Napoleon's army for its 1798 invasion of Egypt. Though this relationship was highly profitable, it eventually led to trouble. In 1827, when France refused to pay the debt it owed for the war effort, the two nations broke off relations. Three years later the French invaded Algeria and made it a colony.

An 18th-century engraving of the city of Algiers and its port. (Picture Collection, The Branch Libraries, The New York Public Library)

MOROCCO—A WORLD APART

In the 16th century the independent kingdom of Morocco occupied much the same territory modern Morocco occupies today. Unified in the early 1500s under the Sa'dids, a clan of Arab nomads, Morocco successfully defended itself from both European and Ottoman incursion until the 20th century. Morocco derived most of its prosperity from trade with West African peoples south of the Sahara and with Europe. Its primary export to the south was salt, for which it received gold, slaves and various other goods. European seafarers on the Mediterranean Sea brought firearms and other manufactured items in exchange for leather goods, slaves and produce. The coastal port cities thrived as centers of trade, but Morocco's king ignored the rural areas, which were subject to attack from Berber nomads.

In order to maintain its independence, Morocco maintained a diplomatic balance between Spanish and Ottoman interests. The navies of Spain and Turkey fought for control of the Moroccan coast throughout the 16th century, with the Turks finally withdrawing in 1571. Although Spain had access to Morocco, pirates known as the Salé controlled local waters and preyed on merchant ships. In 1578 the Portuguese launched an invasion that failed, paving the way for the ascent of a powerful Moroccan leader named Ahmad Al-Mansur. Al-Mansur cultivated British friendship as a defense against ongoing Spanish threats and as a means of access to firearms. He sought to develop local industries and determined to transform Morocco into a mercantile giant.

Al-Mansur attempted to take control of the lucrative trans-Saharan gold trade by invading the West African empire of Songhai in 1591. Under his command thousands of soldiers, camels and horses made the 20-week march across the desert. While only half arrived in fighting condition, the Moroccans' discipline and superior weaponry allowed them to take Songhai and its fabled capital of Timbuktu. The conquest, however, seriously disrupted trade, and Al-Mansur found that the venture was not nearly as profitable as he had hoped. He also had difficulty controlling a reluctant colony 1,000 miles away and was forced to devote tens of thousands of troops to the effort. After Al-Mansur's death in 1603, Morocco's new leaders abandoned Songhai.

Following a period of internal disorder in Morocco, the Alawid dynasty took the crown late in the 17th century. The Alawids built an army of slaves from the Sahara to protect the kingdom's borders and secure the Saharan trade routes. On the seas, Morocco engaged in piracy and legitimate commerce until the 19th century, when it began to worry about growing European influence. The sultan declared an isolationist policy under which Moroccan subjects were prohibited from traveling abroad and foreign visitors were restricted to the coastal cities of Mogador and Tangier. At the same time, the nation's sultans struggled to gain control over uncooperative subjects in outlying areas, to repel persistent nomad raiders and to quell a budding rebellion among religious leaders. Despite these conflicts, Morocco was able to resist foreign colonizers until 1912.

THE SAHARA—BERBERS, BEDOUINS, TUAREG

Little is known of the nomadic peoples of the Sahara in the years between 1500 and 1900. The original inhabitants of the area were Berbers, dark-skinned Caucasians who include the Tuareg. When Arabs swept into North Africa during the Great Age of Islam (7th through 13th centuries), bedouins (Arab nomads) migrated from the deserts of the Arabian peninsula and settled in the Sahara. Most of the Sahara's nomadic peoples practiced Islam, though the Tuareg adhered to their traditional faith well into the modern era. Nomadic herders populated the desert in small, scattered groups, occasionally visiting the few permanent settlements established at oases.

Berber nomads intermarried with Arab bedouins, forming a Muslim society based on clans of about 100 people each. Each clan governed itself, seeking contact with other clans only in times of war. They raised sheep, goats and cattle, moving frequently to fresh pastures. Although they were practicing Muslims, their version of Islam included elements of traditional religions. Women generally had more status than in the settled Muslim world. During the 19th century a fundamentalist Islamic movement, begun by an Algerian religious leader known as Muhammad al-Sanusi, became popular among some nomad groups. *Zawiyas*, or religious centers, sprang up across a large portion of the Sahara, while *ikhwan*, or religious leaders, organized agricultural and commercial activity in the region. The unifying effects of the movement

A view of oases in the Sahara desert of northern Africa. (Picture Collection, The Branch Libraries, The New York Public Library)

allowed the nomads to resist pressures from the established governments to the north as well as from French, British and Turkish interlopers who sought to control the Sahara.

Setting greater store by their ancestral customs than they did by Islam, the Tuareg did not join the Sanusi movement in large numbers. They continued the matriarchal traditions of their culture, according to which women determine the lines of inheritance in a clan. Tuareg culture was highly structured and divided into several tiers of status. The noble clans ruled over scattered Tuareg confederations, which consisted of vassal clans that administered daily life, worker clans that served as artisans and slave clans that carried out menial tasks. The cohesive religious and social forms of the Tuareg, as well as their nomadic way of life, allowed them to maintain their autonomy even as European colonizers laid claim to Africa late in the 19th century.

THE TRADING
CITY-STATES
AND KINGDOMS
OF EAST AFRICA

Perhaps more than any other part of the continent, East Africa thrived on commerce. The region's rich natural resources, which included fertile farmland, vast grazing territories, abundant mineral deposits and a large elephant population, provided its people with ample means to cultivate, mine and hunt products for trade. Migration, war and exploration opened a wide network of routes along which merchants traveled from one settlement to another, linking the kingdoms of the interior with the ports of the coast. Along East Africa's long Indian Ocean coastline, dozens of cities prospered from trade with Arab and Indian seafarers, who imported the luxuries of the East in exchange for the raw materials and manufactured goods of Africa.

Although the peoples of East Africa shared an interest in commerce, the region was culturally diverse during the four centuries preceding European colonization. To the north, the Ethiopians made up Africa's only Christian nation, following customs and speaking languages all their own under centralized rule. The peoples of the central and

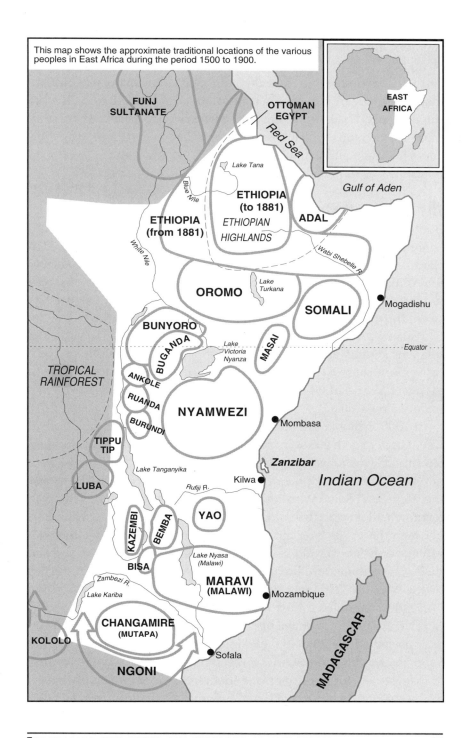

This map shows the approximate traditional locations of the various peoples in East Africa during the period 1500 to 1900.

EAST AFRICA

FUNJ SULTANATE

OTTOMAN EGYPT

Red Sea

Lake Tana

Blue Nile

Gulf of Aden

ETHIOPIA (to 1881)

ETHIOPIA (from 1881)

ETHIOPIAN HIGHLANDS

ADAL

White Nile

Wabi Shebelle R.

OROMO

Lake Turkana

SOMALI

Mogadishu

BUNYORO

Lake Victoria Nyanza

MASAI

Equator

BUGANDA

TROPICAL RAINFOREST

ANKOLE

RUANDA

NYAMWEZI

BURUNDI

TIPPU TIP

Mombasa

LUBA

Lake Tanganyika

Zanzibar

Kilwa

Indian Ocean

Rufiji R.

KAZEMBI

BEMBA

YAO

BISA

Lake Nyasa (Malawi)

Zambezi R.

MARAVI (MALAWI)

Lake Kariba

Mozambique

MADAGASCAR

CHANGAMIRE (MUTAPA)

KOLOLO

Sofala

NGONI

southern interior, meanwhile, were largely Bantu-speaking followers of various traditional religions, living in social units that ranged from very small to quite large. And along the coast, the inhabitants of more than three dozen independent city-states, each ruled by a Muslim sultan, spoke Swahili and devoted themselves to Islam. Apart from these coastal cities, which absorbed Arab, Indian and European influences via trade and conquest, East Africa's many cultures developed relatively free of outside interference until the 19th century.

THE CHRISTIAN KINGDOM OF ETHIOPIA

Built on the ashes of the ancient culture of Aksum, Ethiopia is sub-Saharan Africa's oldest existing state. Its kings claimed lineage that started with Menelik I, the fabled son of the biblical king Solomon and the Arabian queen of Sheba. By the 4th century the nation converted to Christianity, remaining faithful to that religion even when Islam swept through North Africa and isolated Ethiopia from the rest of the Christian world. The country may well owe its longevity to its strong religious identity and its centralized government, for despite periodic disruptions these two elements provided unity in the face of foreign threats. Over its 2,000-year history, Ethiopia has spent only five years under colonial rule.

In 1500 Ethiopia extended from the southern reaches of Ottoman Egypt in the north almost to Lake Turkana in the south. Its rulers and citizens alike were weary from a century of war with the Muslim state of Adal, which lay to the east, between the Ethiopian Highlands and the Red Sea. Some Muslim merchants had penetrated Ethiopian territory and set up a few sultanates, and there were frequent conflicts between these Muslims and their Christian neighbors. Adal took advantage of Ethiopia's momentary weakness in 1526, launching a jihad (holy war) with modern firearms supplied by Ottoman Turks. Overrun by the Muslims, Ethiopia struggled to expel them until 1543, when Portuguese mariners came to their aid and beat back the "infidels."

Like all Europe, Portugal saw Ethiopia as a Christian ally in Muslim and "pagan" Africa. Due to the influence of the Ethiopian church, the nation had certain educational and cultural features that were familiar to Europeans. But the Ethiopians adhered to Monophysite Christianity, an ancient Egyptian sect that the Roman Catholic church deemed heretical. After routing Adal in 1543, the Portuguese set up Catholic missions in Ethiopia, hoping to convert the population to European Christianity. The Ethiopians ignored their efforts.

Because the war between Ethiopia and Adal depopulated both lands and left them unable to defend their borders, the way was opened for immigration by outsiders. To the south, in the area surrounding Lake Turkana, a group of cattle-herding peoples known as the Oromo saw the opportunity to move their livestock to new grazing lands in thinly populated southern Ethiopia. Oromo clans moved northward as their cattle holdings grew and were in turn pushed farther north by groups that followed. Although the migration was generally peaceful, the Oromo forced Ethiopian farmers off their land, and by 1600 so many Oromo had arrived that they made up the majority of southern Ethiopia's population. Some Oromo converted to Christianity and others converted to Islam; some settled as farmers and others remained pastoralists.

Ethiopia's system of government consisted of a central emperor and his court, who ruled over a federation of smaller kingdoms headed by lesser kings. Each king collected taxes from his people and in turn paid tribute to the emperor. Early in the 17th century Oromo was officially recognized as one of Ethiopia's constituent kingdoms, joining the other southern kingdoms as a relatively independent province. Until the middle of the 19th century, Ethiopian power was concentrated in the north. Aside from annual tribute requirements, the north had little influence on the south. The emperor and northern kings devoted most of their energies to the highly profitable slave trade, in which they sold their own subjects to Egyptians, Ottoman Turks and Arabs.

During the 18th century the Ethiopian emperor established his capital at Gondar, high in the mountains near Lake Tana. The magnificent city was built with the wealth collected from the territorial kings and gleaned from the trade in highly prized Ethiopian slaves. Focusing on the accumulation of riches, the emperors of the 18th and 19th centuries left the defense of the provinces to the local kings. Some of these kings built fierce armies, and Ethiopia began to fragment into smaller kingdoms. Then, in 1855, a king from a western province used his soldiers to seize the imperial throne in Gondar. Crowning himself Tewodros (Theodore) II, the new emperor set out to restore the unity and strength of the Ethiopian empire.

Tewodros established a professional central government and appointed salaried governors and judges to oversee the provinces. He banned hereditary rule in the provinces and abolished the special privileges of the church. He also expanded the military and trained it in modern techniques, using it to quash rebellions by the old provincial kings who protested against his reforms. The emperor's arrest of two British diplomats on minor charges in 1868 led to his downfall. When he refused to release the officials, Britain sent 30,000 troops to free them. Tewodros, increasingly unpopular, was unable to rally the support he needed from his people, some of whom joined with the British against him. He suffered a humiliating defeat and committed suicide.

One of the Ethiopian military officers who fought Tewodros used weapons supplied by the British to claim the throne after the emperor's death. Crowned Johannes (John) IV, he returned many powers to the church and to the hereditary provincial kings, who had been weakened under Tewodros. These moves bolstered his strength by winning the loyalties of Ethiopia's elite, and he was able to repel a subsequent attempt by Ottoman Egypt to expand into Ethiopian territory. When he died in 1889 Johannes was succeeded by Menelik II, a powerful southern leader. Menelik secured Ethiopia's place in the modern world, first by expanding the empire into Sidama, Somali and independent Oromo lands, then by handing Italian invaders a stunning defeat at the battle of Adowa in 1896. This display of military might discouraged other would-be European colonizers from trying to claim Ethiopia when they divided up the rest of Africa.

ON THE SHORES OF LAKE VICTORIA

South of the Ethiopian, Oromo and Somali kingdoms lay a land bounded on the east by the Indian Ocean and on the west by the vast tropical rain forest of the Congo (Zaire) River. At the center of this territory was Lake Victoria, the third-largest lake in the world, and around this lake half a dozen distinct societies thrived. Because no written language developed in the area, current knowledge of its peoples comes from archaeological finds and the oral history traditions that reach back to 1400 and are still carried on today.

Most of these cultures relied heavily on cattle herding for their livelihood, basing their diet on meat and milk and migrating occasionally in a seminomadic pattern. Many groups, especially those closer to the coast, practiced agriculture, raising such crops as grain, coffee and cotton. Everywhere, people mined rich deposits of copper, iron, tin and gold and traded both with neighboring peoples and with traveling merchants from the coast.

The group most closely associated with the region's cattle-herding traditions are the Masai, who still live much as they have for centuries. In search of grazing land for their herds, the Masai migrated into present-day Kenya from the north in the 16th and 17th centuries. Because their beliefs included the understanding that all the world's cattle belonged to them, they evicted the area's previous occupants and claimed their cattle and lands. The Masai structured their society according to age, assigning duties accordingly: Young men served as soldiers and herdsmen while elders governed each village by council. Although they conducted frequent cattle raids on nearby pastoralists, they traded peacefully with local farmers for food. Their commercial activities seldom went further, though, and the Masai generally remained aloof from the trading and slaving turmoil that racked East Africa in the 19th century.

The largest and most powerful culture in the vicinity of Lake Victoria was that of the Bunyoro, founded by migrants from the Sudan and Ethiopia. In the 1400s the new arrivals introduced their traditions and subdued the area's original inhabitants, evicting some from their land and assuming sovereignty over others. One tradition the migrants brought with them was the age-grade structure of their society, similar to that of the Masai. In this system, each clan or village was organized according to the ages of its members. There might be three simple gradations (for example, children, young adults, elders) or many more subtle ones indicating each person's status. Age grades determined the occupation, behavior and even dress of the Bunyoro. The system came into common use throughout the interior of East Africa.

Rich in iron and salt and well suited to coffee-growing, the land the Bunyoro lived on supported a mixed economy of farming, hunting and herding. A confederation of chiefdoms paid tribute to a single king and supplied him with military regiments for raids on nearby peoples. Ever in search of booty, the kings of Bunyoro raided the neighboring Ankole, Rwanda and Buganda. This focus on military activity, coupled with

A Masai woman in traditional dress, Kenya. (Picture Collection, The Branch Libraries, The New York Public Library)

increasing difficulty in their campaigns—especially those against the Ankole—weakened the Bunyoro in the 18th and 19th centuries. At the same time, the Buganda to the southeast grew in power and soon controlled the Bunyoro's access to vital trading routes.

Scattered along the northwest coast of Lake Victoria, the Buganda lived on fertile land well suited to agriculture. Bananas, plantains and coffee were specialties and grew almost without tending. The Buganda also manufactured barkcloth, a luxury item that brought good prices when they started trading with Swahili caravans from Africa's east coast in the 18th century. Small, prosperous and densely populated, Buganda territory was ruled by a single king starting in the 1700s. The king granted land to nobles, who taxed the farmers and herdsmen and paid tribute to the monarch. Using tax revenues to build a disciplined army and a network of roads that linked all parts of the territory to the capital, the Buganda rulers maintained tight control over their land. By 1800 the Buganda were more powerful than the Bunyoro.

Southwest of Bunyoro and Buganda, three smaller societies peopled the uppermost reaches of the Nile. The Ankole, Rwanda and Burundi developed three-tiered societies in which a ruling class of cattle owners made up perhaps one-tenth of the population, a middle class of farmers and artisans represented about 85 percent and a slave class represented around 5 percent. Hunters and potters, the slaves were short and dark, while the middle class was of medium height and color. Taller and lighter skinned than the others, and later known to Europeans as the Watutsi, the ruling class hired those below them to herd their cattle. They taxed the farmers, who provided them with tobacco and food, and conducted business with the traders who passed through their territory starting in the 18th century.

The trading activities of the Bunyoro, Buganda, Ankole, Rwanda and Burundi came to depend on the Nyamwezi, who inhabited the region now known as Tanzania. Originally a widely dispersed set of small chiefdoms made up of farmers and pastoralists, the Nyamwezi developed into a powerful nation of professional traders in the late 18th century. Increasing trade between the seacoast and the interior took caravans through the heart of Nyamwezi territory, and the local people learned how to profit from the traffic. They pioneered efficient routes and gained a position as "middlemen" between the coastal merchants and the peoples who lived farther into the interior. Products from the coast, such as cloth, luxury goods and firearms, passed into Nyamwezi hands in exchange for iron, salt, ivory and slaves from the interior. As entrepreneurs, the Nyamwezi grew rich and powerful.

In the 19th century, however, the Nyamwezi faced new challenges. The huge profits to be made from the heavy demand for ivory and slaves caused Swahili from the coast and Egyptians from the north to press into Nyamwezi territory in an attempt to control the trading routes.

The capital of Buganda. (Peter Newark's Historical Pictures)

Local kings, newly armed with modern weapons, rebuffed the invaders in bloody battles. But the slave raids and massacres of elephant herds continued at the hands of the local people, and coastal merchants continued to press for commercial power as well as political control. The struggles brought instability to the entire region, leaving it vulnerable to European greed at the end of the century.

NORTH AND SOUTH OF THE ZAMBEZI

One of the principal geographic features of southern East Africa, the Zambezi River flows across the region and drains into the Mozambique Channel, which separates the Indian Ocean island of Madagascar from the mainland. From 1500 to 1900 the river served as a main trading route for the people of the area, and dozens of trading settlements dotted its banks. A number of great cultures prospered in the hilly country north and south of the river, raising crops, herding cattle, mining gold, hunting ivory and trading among themselves as well as with Swahili and Portuguese merchants from the seacoast. Until the 19th century, trade provided a measure of stability to the region, allowing large populations to obtain the diverse goods they needed to survive. Thereafter, the area experienced political and economic upheavals largely as a result of contact with Europeans.

The plateau south of the Zambezi was home to Torwa, Mutapa and Changamire, three dynasties that were the heirs to the empire of Great Zimbabwe. Great Zimbabwe, known for the elaborate stone enclosures that protected its cattle and wealthy citizens, thrived between 1200 and 1450. Ruled by divine kings who also served as religious leaders, the dynasties that succeeded Great Zimbabwe consisted of numerous minor chiefdoms that paid tribute to the central government. The dynasties expanded their power and wealth by conquering additional small kingdoms, many of which were unstable because of frequent war and a lack of clear succession to their thrones. The Torwa, Mutapa and Changamire sometimes had difficulty controlling their far-flung provinces.

Torwa and Mutapa rose simultaneously in the late 1400s, conquering the peoples of the Zambezi River valley to secure supplies of food, salt and gold plus access to the river trading routes. They traded gold and ivory with merchant caravans from the coast and occasionally had to defend themselves against outsiders' efforts to take control of their territory. In 1571 Mutapa repelled a Portuguese invasion; in 1623, however, the Maravi people from the northeast succeeded in penetrating Mutapa territory. Portuguese settlers known as *prazeros* filtered into weakened Torwa and Mutapa throughout the 1600s, claiming large estates called prazos and oppressing the local people. The prazeros intermarried with Africans and pursued their own interests, independent of Portuguese control. The local people asked their legitimate kings for protection from the expoitation, and the rulers built strong private armies that fought the prazeros.

One such army was headed by a warrior who called himself Changamire. With the backing of soldiers he named *rozvi* (the destroyers), Changamire conquered Torwa and Mutapa in the 1680s and proceeded to eject the prazeros from the area. By 1696 the Changamire empire was firmly established south of the Zambezi. The empire developed an efficient system of administration and maintained the rozvi as a means of keeping order and collecting tribute in the form of food, cattle, tobacco, gold, ivory and cloth. All important activities, such as ivory carving, gold mining and weaving, fell under royal control, as did trade. Portuguese merchants were not permitted in Changamire territory, and all transactions were heavily taxed. Rich and powerful, Changamire dominated the region until the 19th century.

North of the Zambezi around Lake Malawi, meanwhile, lived the Maravi (Malawi), a people ruled by a loose association of chiefdoms. Their name meant "people of fire" and referred to their use of fire in religious rituals. The Maravi herded cattle for meat and milk; for the purposes of trade they also hunted and carved ivory, grew and wove cotton and mined and worked iron, copper and gold. Strong enough to resist Portuguese invasions in the 16th century, Maravi culture peaked in the years between 1600 and 1650, when a chief named Kalonga Masula ruled. Maravi declined after his death, leaving a large tract of East Africa open to slave raids and trade wars in the 19th century.

The Kazembi, Bisa and Bemba occupied the lands west of Lake Malawi, making their living as professional traders and raiders. As trade expanded in the 19th century, the centrally located Kazembi served as go-betweens for traders from Africa's east and west coasts. They imported firearms, wool and cotton cloth, shells and beads for local consumption and exported copper, salt, ivory and slaves to the coasts. The Bisa carried on trade with east-coast merchants, while the Bemba thrived as pirates who raided trading caravans and settlements. To their northeast, across Lake Malawi, the Yao grew rich as full-time long-distance traders. After converting to Islam, the Yao profited from friendly relations with the Muslim entrepreneurs of the coast.

Booming demand for ivory and slaves raised the stakes of commerce and made southern East Africa a violent place in the 19th century. Prazeros pushed into Maravi territory, formed slave armies of local people and set themselves up as chiefs. Their captive soldiers, called *chikunda*, collected taxes, raided settlements and caravans and hunted ivory and slaves for trade. Led by an Omani Arab sultan based on the island of Zanzibar, coastal Swahili and Arab traders penetrated the interior at the same time in search of ivory and slaves. Huge caravans of up to 1,000 people drove through the area, establishing permanent settlements and raiding local villages. In addition, starting in the 1830s, the Ngoni people flooded into East Africa, fleeing violence in the south. Highly militarized groups of Ngoni spread throughout the region, plundering and absorbing those they encountered.

Conflicts among Africans and outsiders ravaged the region's traditional cultures in the 19th century. Entire villages were kidnapped as slaves; thousands of elephants were slaughtered for their tusks. When Europeans arrived, they found crumbling societies and internal chaos. Only the military expertise of the Ngoni allowed the people of East Africa's interior to resist colonization as long as they did.

THE SWAHILI CITY-STATES OF THE COAST

Strung along Africa's east coast, from Mogadishu in present-day Somalia to Sofala in present-day Mozambique, about 40 port cities linked Africa with Asia and the Middle East in the centuries preceding colonization. A strip of dry, inhospitable land separated the coast from the interior, serving for many years as a barrier that kept the culture of the coast quite distinct from that of the interior. The people lived in large towns built of coral stone, each of which was independently ruled by a Muslim sultan. Indeed, Islam featured prominently in every aspect of coastal life, from architecture and politics to diet and language. Imported by Arab traders who settled in the area and intermarried with

TIPPU TIP,
SWAHILI TRADER AND SULTAN

One of the more remarkable Swahili traders of East Africa was Hamed bin Muhammed, commonly known as Tippu Tip. Born about 1830 in Zanzibar, this entrepreneur of mixed Swahili, Arab and Nyamwezi ancestry started his hunting and raiding career among the Nyamwezi in the 1860s. He set up a permanent base on the Lualaba (upper Congo) River and united other Swahili traders operating in the area, dubbing himself the sultan of Utetera. Tippu Tip maintained good relations with Zanzibar as well as with the Nyamwezi chiefs through whom he traded with the coast. He hunted elephants for ivory and raided local villages for food and captives, trading ivory for guns.

During the 1870s Tippu Tip maintained a large army and expanded his "kingdom" eastward to the shores of Lake Tanganyika, southward to Lunda-Luba territory and northwestward down the upper Congo basin. He built roads, plantations and an extensive trade network that brought him immense profits. Slaves taken in raids throughout the area were used as concubines, as porters for Tippu Tip's trading caravans and as plantation workers who grew sugarcane, rice and maize (corn) for consumption and exchange. Tippu Tip traded surplus slaves for ivory, his main export.

Tippu Tip became one of the most powerful figures in the western reaches of East Africa, even meeting with famed British explorer Sir Henry Morton Stanley when the adventurer arrived in the upper Congo area in 1877. Aware of European interest in his territory, Tippu Tip tried to deflect colonization by claiming his kingdom was part of the Omani empire ruled by the sultan of Zanzibar. Europe did not recognize the sultan's sovereignty, however, and Tippu Tip's kingdom became part of the Congo Free State in 1887. Tippu Tip served as governor of his province until 1890, when he retired to the coast a rich but defeated man.

Africans, Islam provided a cultural bond between the city-states. The local language, Swahili or Kiswahili, was a mix of Bantu and Arabic. A written form developed, using the Arabic alphabet.

Some of the coastal trading cities, such as Zanzibar and Pemba, were actually located on small islands just off the mainland. Whether on an island or the mainland, they owed their survival to the monsoon winds of the Indian Ocean. The winds blew steadily toward Africa during the winter, bringing ships from India and the Arabian peninsula. During the summer the winds blew steadily away from Africa, sending the continent's exports eastward. Seafaring merchants rode the monsoon winds to Africa for spices, incense, ivory, slaves and gold and brought cloth, porcelain and luxury goods in exchange. The cities of Kilwa and Sofala were the most important ports for this trade.

Because peace was good for business, the Swahili traders rarely fought among themselves. They sometimes raided interior kingdoms or were raided in turn, but they seldom translated commercial rivalries into military ones. In 1505, however, the Portuguese attacked the towns of the southern coast and established forts there to control trade on the Indian Ocean. The northern towns managed to resist for a while, but by 1599 the whole coast was under Portuguese control. Coastal life continued much as it had before; now however, Portuguese governors rather than Muslim sultans collected taxes. Under the Portuguese, the slave trade mushroomed in the 18th century. Some Portuguese settlers broke away from government authority, moved into the interior as prazeros and established slave-based plantations there.

The Portuguese held onto the East African coast until late in the 17th century, when Arabs from Oman began to encroach. The Omanis took the crucial city of Mombasa in 1698 and soon dominated the northern coast. Between 1822 and 1837 Seyyid Said bin Sultan of Oman conquered most of the remaining Portuguese outposts and established himself on Zanzibar as the ruler of the Omani empire. He developed the local cultivation of cloves and other expensive spices and sent large caravans into the mainland for goods. Highly organized and efficient, Said's Swahili and Arab traders established permanent posts in the interior and exported large amounts of ivory and slaves, but Said was unable to fulfill his ambition of gaining political control of the region. Before long, in fact, he lost the coast to new European arrivals.

THE RICH
TRADITIONS OF
WEST AFRICA

Until the European nations divided Africa into colonies in the late 19th and early 20th centuries, West Africa was in many respects the center of black African culture. There, in medieval and early modern times, rose the great civilizations of the sub-Saharan golden age: the wealthy, vibrant empires of Ghana and Mali. Even after these societies faded, West Africa was home to numerous smaller states that developed sophisticated political, economic and religious structures. Most dazzling, though, were the artistic traditions of these cultures. Stunning sculpture, music, dance, metalwork, weaving, needlework, basketry, pottery, architecture and other expressions flowed from the hearts and hands of the region's artists. Although outsiders at first considered African art a mere curiosity, it is now ranked among the world's finest artistic achievements.

West Africa's cultural flowering took place in a geographically diverse region that stretches along the continent's Atlantic coast from the Sahara desert in the north to the Kalahari Desert in the south. The people there inhabited three distinct zones: the strip of savannah, known as the Sudan, just south of the Sahara; the vast tract of tropical

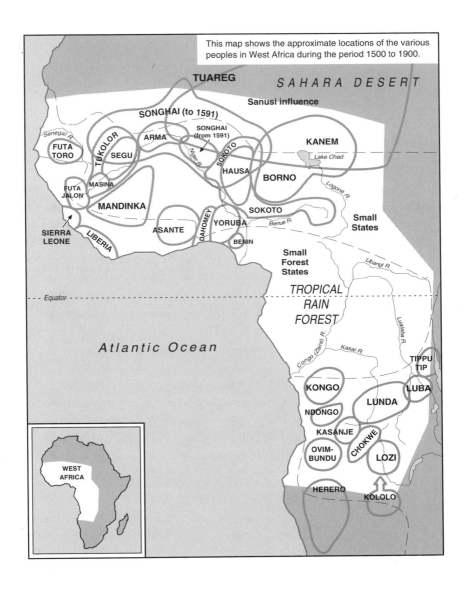

This map shows the approximate locations of the various peoples in West Africa during the period 1500 to 1900.

rain forest known as Guinea (not to be confused with the present-day country of Guinea); and the savannah land south of the rain forest, in the area now occupied by Angola. Along with their arts, the peoples of West Africa established an efficient network of trade routes that supported a thriving economy long before the intrusion of European merchants and slavers. After the European arrival, the slave trade swept the region, consuming entire societies and leaving others severely weakened. Indeed, West Africa was the area of the continent hardest hit by slavery, making it easy prey for European nations intent on expanding their colonial empires.

THE SUDAN

The early 1500s saw the peak of the empire of Songhai in the West African Sudan. Successor to Ghana and Mali, Songhai was based in the region watered by the middle Niger River. Its imperial influence extended across the entire western Sudan and well into the Sahara. Songhai controlled trade between the gold-mining peoples of Guinea to the south and the trans-Saharan traders who linked the Sudan with North Africa. The empire, especially its two major cities, Timbuktu and Gao, grew rich on the profits of commerce in gold, salt, kola nuts and slaves. Much of the money went to building a powerful military, which expanded the empire by conquest and brought numerous tribute-paying kingdoms under centralized rule.

Largely Muslim as a result of its close contact with North Africa, Songhai often justified its raids on non-Muslim neighbors as *jihads* or holy wars. The king removed conquered provincial rulers from authority and appointed nonhereditary governors in their place, who were responsible for collecting taxes and raising armies. Farming, hunting and fishing, the main activities of the empire's ordinary folk, continued much as they had for centuries, though the people were subject to heavy taxation, forced military service and slave raids. Few of the common people converted to Islam.

During the 16th century Songhai faltered as drought, disease and a series of internal power struggles sapped its strength. Meanwhile, the nearby states of Borno and Kanem, and the Hausa people in the empire's eastern reaches, began competing for trade long dominated by Songhai. In the 1580s civil war broke out in Songhai, making it vulnerable to attack from outsiders. Morocco took advantage of the situation in 1591, launching an invasion with a highly trained force equipped with the latest European firearms. Songhai, which had failed to modernize its army, fell quickly and its empire disintegrated. Guerrilla resistance and internal chaos eventually discouraged the Moroc-

An 18th-century engraving of the fabled city of Timbuktu in modern-day Mali.
(Picture Collection, The Branch Libraries, The New York Public Library)

can intruders, who left the area early in the 1700s. Songhai was no more, and a set of independent kingdoms, such as Segu and Arma, rose in its place.

The mercantile vacuum left by the decline of Songhai was quickly filled by Borno, Kanem and the Hausa. Situated to the west of Lake Chad, Borno counted Kanem, to the east of Lake Chad, among its provinces. Until the 14th century, Borno had been a tributary state of Kanem, but by 1500 Borno had become the stronger of the two states. Borno, a Muslim state, was headed by rulers called *mais*. Throughout the 1500s the mais led a series of jihads to suppress peasant uprisings and take captives to sell as slaves.

Growing prosperity allowed Borno to update its weaponry and military techniques late in the 16th century in order to raid neighboring states and collect tribute from them. After this period of expansion, Borno and Kanem entered a peaceful period during which the arts and sciences flourished under Islamic influence. Borno retained its dominant position until the 19th century, when it was attacked in a jihad by the Fulani people of the Sokoto empire to the west. Strict Muslims seeking to broaden their territory, the Fulani considered Borno and Kanem fair game. When they invaded, however, one of Kanem's military leaders stepped forward to pursuade the Fulani that Borno and Kanem were already Muslim. His ability to stop the jihad by diplomatic means elevated Kanem to a leadership role in the region once again.

The Hausa people were not as successful in fending off the Fulani. Organized as a set of independent city-states, the Hausa thrived along the lower Niger River starting about 1400. Each city-state centered around a walled city protected by an elaborate wooden stockade. Slave labor built and maintained the city walls and contributed to the cultivation of food. The peasantry engaged in agriculture and manufacturing, while the ruling class controlled busy trade routes that channeled gold, slaves, salt and manufactured goods between the forest states of Guinea and the North African states across the Sahara. In the course of trade with trans-Saharan caravans, Hausa leaders converted to Islam. They organized their city-state governments into elaborate bureaucracies that ran according to Islamic law.

From 1500 to 1800 the Hausa city-states enjoyed relative prosperity, although rivalries among the numerous states sometimes led to war. During the 18th century, however, the peasantry suffered increasingly harsh taxation and slave raids that previously had been directed only at non-Hausa peoples. Once the Hausa masses started converting to Islam in the 18th century, they began criticizing their rulers. The internal strife opened opportunities for foreign aggressors; when the Fulani launched a jihad against the Hausa early in the 19th century, the small states fell one after another. In 1808 the last Hausa city surrendered to the Fulani.

Before the 18th century the Fulani, who were also known as the Fulbe, lived as nomadic cattle-herders across the entire Sudan west of Lake Chad. The only pastoral people in the region, they lived compatibly among the settled agricultural societies, independent of the authority of any ruler. Their way of life and their Caucasian features set them apart from those among whom they lived, marking them as outsiders. When their herds grew and they sought more grazing land in the 18th century, their neighbors grew resentful. The Fulani turned to Islam for a sense of unity and security and soon ranked among Africa's most learned Muslim scholars.

Before long the Fulani initiated jihads against the non-Muslims around them, using the wars to expand their grazing territory. Between 1725 and 1750 they conquered the Futa Jalon, who lived near the sources of the Senegal and Niger rivers; from 1769 to 1776 they waged a successful jihad against the Futa Toro within the curve of the Senegal. Both wars provided numerous captives to be sold as slaves to European traders and led to the formation of new Muslim states. To the east, jihads against the remains of Songhai, the Hausa, the Yoruba and eastern Borno brought a large area under Fulani control. The defeated kingdoms were transformed into Muslim emirates that united into a confederation known as the Sokoto Caliphate. Along with Islam, literacy spread to a wider segment of the population. Trade with Muslim merchants who traversed the Sahara brought wealth to the rulers of the caliphate.

In 1818 another Fulani jihad established the state of Masina along the upper Niger, between Futa Jalon and Segu. Masina and Segu next received unwanted attention from a Muslim leader named al-Hajj 'Umar. Born in Futa Toro, Umar had moved to Futa Jalon and acquired many followers faithful to his vision of Islam. Umar started a jihad against Masina in the 1840s and gradually pushed down the Niger through Segu. His empire, called Tukolor, fanned out from the riverbanks for miles into the savannah on either side, reaching its greatest extent in the early 1860s. Umar forced his subjects to convert to his brand of Islam and, ignoring the necessity of establishing a strong government, pressed on to further conquest. Before he could succeed, he died in 1864. Without Umar, Tukolor remained unstable, subject to frequent rebellions and power struggles.

South of Tukolor, another Muslim empire rose in the 19th century. This one had nothing to do with the Fulani, however. Samori Toure, a member of a powerful non-Muslim trading family that maintained a private army, established the Mandinka empire on his own. He converted to Islam as a young man and determined to augment his family's control of trade in the western Sudan. Between 1865 and 1875 he conquered the area east of Futa Jalon, establishing a Muslim trading kingdom. That kingdom became an empire as Toure continued his push north and east. Motivated by Islamic principles, Toure promoted education and trade in his empire, which reached its greatest extent in the 1880s. Captives taken in battle were added to the army rather than sold as slaves, and modern firearms were imported to strengthen the military. The Mandinka empire enjoyed prosperity and unity until it encountered the French in the 1890s.

GUINEA AND THE RAIN FOREST

Clustered in the forest along Africa's Atlantic coast, between the land of the Futa Jalon and the Niger River delta, lay the greatest concentration of art-producing peoples on the continent. The area now occupied by the countries of Guinea, Sierra Leone, Liberia and Ivory Coast was inhabited by a number of peoples who lived in tiny or decentralized chiefdoms and who supported themselves by hunting, fishing and some trade. To their west were four mighty cultures with sophisticated governmental systems: Asante/Ashanti, Dahomey, Yoruba and Benin. Because Islam did not penetrate the Guinea forest until very late, the region's people practiced their traditional religions, from which sprang the remarkable art for which Africa is known today. But until the second half of 20th century, Europeans were more interested in the slaves, gold and ivory they could take from the area than they were in the artistic genius of its people.

The Asante, also known as the Ashanti, consisted of several Akan peoples who lived in independent states until the 1670s. Like many other African peoples, the Akan traced their heritage matrilineally, through the bloodlines of women rather than those of men. Inheritance of wealth and position depended on the ancestry of the mother, although men for the most part governed daily life. In the 1670s one such man, a clan chief with a reputation for great military skill, united a number of Akan chiefdoms into a larger, stronger state and started raiding neighboring peoples. By 1700 Asante conquered most of the kingdoms that owned the forest's rich gold fields, and by 1750 Asante covered an area equivalent to most of present-day Ghana. Rather than submitting to the Asante, the Baule people, some of Africa's finest musicians, moved out of the empire and to the west.

The Asante kings centralized government administration in the late 18th century, abolishing the hereditary chiefdoms of its tributary states and appointing governors and tax collectors in their place. Each province provided soldiers for the royal army and paid tribute to the central treasury, usually in the form of gold. Gold mining was done by slaves under the direction of provincial governors, while many common folk panned for the precious metal in rivers and streams. Most of the gold that did not go toward taxes was purchased by agents of the king, who gave other metals, firearms, salt and cloth in exchange. In this way, as well as through sales of war captives as slaves, the Asante court grew wealthy. The capital city, Kumasi, became a center of politics and religion, a bustling crossroads that attracted merchants, artisans and scholars.

To the east, the kingdom of Dahomey established a highly unified state on more lightly forested territory. Founded early in the 1500s, Dahomey organized as a centralized state in 1650, under an absolute monarchy. The country was divided into six districts plus the capital city of Abomey, all ruled by a single hereditary king. All government officials—the police chief, the tax collector, the army commander, the minister of agriculture and the like—were appointed by the king. To monitor the activities of his staff, the king sent his wives throughout the country as his representatives. All the people of Dahomey lived there only by permission of the king, for he owned all the land and merely loaned it to his subjects for their use. The stature of the Dahomeyan king was further reflected in the practice of making annual human sacrifices in his honor.

The highly disciplined army of Dahomey, which included a large contingent of formidable female warriors, fought frequent wars of expansion. Captives taken in battle were sold as slaves, and the pro-ceeds were used to purchase firearms for the military. Dahomey's pursuit of the slave trade brought it into direct conflict with the Yoruba state of Oyo, which was also an active participant in the slave trade. In 1730 Oyo invaded Dahomey to take control of its slaving enterprises. Dahomey surrendered and agreed to pay tribute to the ruler of Oyo. Although heavily taxed by Oyo the Dahomeyan slave trade remained profitable, and the country thrived as a province of Oyo. It became so robust, in fact, that by 1800 Oyo had no real control there. Dahomey declared its independence in 1818.

Dahomeyan independence heralded the start of a long 19th-century decline for the Yoruba people of Oyo. The Yoruba had first formed an organized state in the 11th century. That kingdom, called Ife, was based in a fertile strip of savannah woodland that penetrated the deep forest. Ife enjoyed a prosperity based on the production of food surpluses and built walled towns for protection against intruders. Relieved of the struggle for survival, the Yoruba of Ife occupied themselves as artists. Commissioned by the king and his court, Yoruban artists crafted beautiful masks, sculpture and ceremonial objects of wood, ivory, terra cotta, bronze, brass and copper. The most respected artists had high status in the community, and lesser artists did their part to ornament the everyday lives of ordinary people.

In the 14th century Ife was replaced by Oyo as the major state of Yorubaland. Oyo inherited the artistic traditions of Ife as well as the security of the walled village and farmland ideal for growing grain. Its leaders, known as *alafins*, claimed near divinity and possessed large numbers of slaves taken in battle. Indeed, Oyo enjoyed great success in war, for it had the region's only cavalry, which could easily defeat foot soldiers. Oyo's wars of conquest extended the kingdom to the coast in the 1600s, giving it access to trade with the European merchants who sailed the Atlantic. Oyo's power and affluence peaked in the middle of the 17th century.

Whenever the Yoruba captured more slaves than could be put to work on the royal farms, they sold their prisoners to seafaring slavers. Oyo's royalty grew rich on the slave trade and used some of their wealth to acquire more horses from the Hausa trading states, which imported them from North Africa. In the 18th century greed began to get the better of certain Yoruba alafins, who started selling their own slaves— and even free citizens—to European slavers. The drain on the labor supply weakened Oyo at the same time that Sokoto jihads among the Hausa dried up the supply of horses. Meanwhile, disruptions in the international slave trade reduced the profitability of Oyo's chief enterprise, causing dissension among the ruling class. Oyo's difficulties paved the way for conquest by Fulani Muslims in the early 1800s. As the century progressed, many Yoruba fled their homeland while others fought with each other and took captives whom they sold into slavery.

The fate of Oyo echoed that of Benin, a small but powerful kingdom in the Niger River delta. A collection of small village chiefdoms surrounding an enormous walled city-state, Benin had a centralized administration that supported a large army. Like the Yoruba, the people

Cast bronze Ife bust from West Africa. (Negative no. 325536. Courtesy Department of Library Services, American Museum of Natural History)

of Benin produced sophisticated artworks, most notably metal sculptures and plaques. Portuguese traders reached Benin in the late 15th century and began exporting pepper, ivory, natural gums and cotton fabric to Europe. Benin's artisans carved ivory pieces for sale to Europeans, perhaps the first example of a foreign market for African art. When civil war broke out in the 1700s, however, Benin's warring chiefs captured and sold many local people into slavery. The practice

AFRICAN ART

Like much of the world's art through the ages, traditional West African art was for the most part inspired by religious belief. Before Islam or Christianity appeared in the region, the peoples of West Africa practiced scores of local religions that can be classified as animism. Animism attributes divinity or spiritual power to animals and inanimate objects such as plants, mountains or the sun. By giving common items and experiences higher meaning, animism incorporates spirituality into most aspects of daily life. As a result, African art meant to affirm religious beliefs was an integral part of everyday activity.

The artists of West Africa created ceremonial music, masks, idols, fetishes, jewelry, crowns and scepters in honor of the gods and of kings, the gods' divine representatives on earth. These items were used at such events as initiations, funerals, hunting and farming rituals, magical rites and celebrations. Cultivated for spiritual purposes, the decorative impulse appeared everywhere, as a love of beauty dictated the form of all kinds of objects. Furniture, drums, knife handles, bowls, pipes, cups, toys, canoes, oars, doors and architecture reflected the West African aesthetic. But today sculpture is widely recognized as the most important contribution of West Africa to the world's artistic heritage. Generally created by male artisans by commission from kings, the region's sculpture was most often executed in wood, although ivory, bone, stone and metal also were used. Many wood sculptures were painted, but time has stripped most of these works of their color.

Because religion was so central to West African art, the introduction of Islam and Christian Protestantism, with their prohibitions against idolatry, usually led to a decline in ancestral art forms. European colonialism hastened that decline by ending support of the arts by local royalty. As modernization progressed and storebought items replaced handmade ones, the market for ancient decorative techniques shrank. Today few West African artists remain to carry on the region's artistic traditions.

had a terrible impact on the kingdom, depopulating the area and demoralizing those who remained there.

To the south and east of Benin, the peoples of the sparsely populated tropical rain forest largely escaped the ravages of the slave trade. Most likely, they did so because the forest protected them from attacks from outsiders and prohibited the development of large states that could exploit common people. The rain forest yielded a living to its inhabitants only grudgingly, requiring a great deal of cooperative effort for survival. Living in small, widely scattered villages, the people farmed, hunted and fished. While the men wandered in search of game, the women tilled the soil, cultivating bananas, sorghum and millet. They also grew cassava and maize (corn), new crops imported from the Americas. Some groups of Pygmies specialized as hunters and traded their catch for produce grown by agricultural clans.

Most rain forest societies were structured by age-set systems, in which people were assigned duties and authority based on their age. Many villages were governed by councils of elders and held town meetings at which every citizen could express an opinion on matters of importance. In some cases, important decisions were made and disputes were resolved by "oracles," spiritual practitioners who could divine the will of the gods. Villages were linked by clubs and secret societies that helped circulate traditions and beliefs among the peoples of the rain forest. Today some of these traditions still exist, having survived in relative isolation from the European slavers, traders, missionaries, explorers and colonizers who destroyed so much of African culture elsewhere.

SOUTH OF THE RAIN FOREST

Starting about 1400, the southern edge of the West African rain forest near the mouth of the Congo River was home to an empire called Kongo. Dozens of small chiefdoms first unified under a king named Manikongo and built a prosperous nation of farmers, potters, metal workers and weavers. The Kongolese were among Africa's most sophisticated makers of cloth. The bright, intricate patterns of their fabrics were recognized and enjoyed by all who acquired them in trade. When Portuguese traders arrived in the area about 1480, they gave the empire's name to the mighty river that runs through the rain forest.

The king of Kongo welcomed the Europeans, hoping to obtain education, training and firearms for his people.

The Portuguese, however, had other plans. They sought slaves for export to Europe and wanted Kongolese assistance in capturing them. A dispute broke out in Kongo between those who favored continued contact with the Portuguese and those who felt it was dangerous. In 1506 the isolationists lost the battle when a Kongolese convert to Christianity seized the throne as King Afonso I and set about developing diplomatic relations with Portugal. Afonso I promoted his people's conversion to Christianity and entered the slave trade by selling war captives to the Portuguese. In order to sustain the slave trade, Portuguese who settled in Kongo encouraged Afonso's successors to continue their wars of expansion. Kongo's aggression against neighboring peoples did not go unavenged. Invading from the east, the Jaga crushed Kongo in 1568. The Portuguese helped Kongo oust the Jaga in 1574 and installed a puppet king who did their bidding. Pursuing the slave trade at the expense of the people, a series of illegitimate rulers allowed the empire to decay. Kongo finally collapsed in the 17th century.

Ndongo, one of Kongo's southern rivals, managed to avoid a similar fate. Led by a ruler called the Ngola, Ndongo maintained a strong army committed to expanding the kingdom's territory. Ndongo entered the slave trade with Portugal in the 1500s, selling its prisoners of war to the slavers. When the Portuguese attempted to take control of Ndongo in the 1580s, fierce resistance by the military combined with the debilitating effects of tropical disease thwarted their efforts. The Portuguese gave up on conquering Ndongo, realizing that the king was already willing to provide a steady supply of slaves taken during the region's almost constant wars. Ndongo prospered until the slave trade declined in the 19th century.

Less directly affected by the slave trade was the Lunda-Luba empire to the east of Ndongo. A confederation of Luba chiefdoms that consolidated under a single king in the 16th century, Lunda grew throughout the 17th and 18th centuries, reaching its greatest extent late in the 1600s. Both the provincial chiefs and the central king had semidivine status. In the small villages that made up the empire, the people farmed, fished, hunted and made goods for trade. Once maize and cassava were imported from the New World, their farms became highly productive and could easily support a rapidly growing population.

Lunda enjoyed stability and security until the 19th century, under a tribute system in which local chiefs taxed the people and paid tribute to the king, who provided protection. The tribute system stimulated long-distance trade with other peoples in such items as raffia cloth, baskets, metal work, iron, copper and salt. Lunda also exported ivory and some slaves to their western neighbors in exchange for woolen cloth and guns from Europe. This trade was conducted through intermediaries from Kasanje, a state that formed in the 17th century. Located in the heart of west-central Africa, the Kasanje traded with and raided all the major societies of the area. During the 1600s and 1700s they were one of the region's most significant suppliers of slaves to European traders.

Slavery played a different role in the lives of the Lozi, who lived on the floodplains of the upper Zambezi River. The Lozi organized under a single king in the 17th century before spreading out to claim control of the entire floodplain region. Flooded each year during the wet season, which lasted from November through March, the plains on either side of the upper Zambezi offered fertile agricultural lands and pastures during the dry season. The king led his people in annual migrations between the flood zone and the drier land to the west, travels that were accompanied by much pomp and ritual. He also supervised the use of slave labor in controlling the floodwaters, tilling the floodplains and building villages.

The predictable cycle of Lozi life was forever disrupted in the 1830s, when the Kololo people of southern Africa fled strife in their homeland and invaded Lozi territory. Claiming southern Lozi lands as their own, the Kololo reduced the local people to slavery. But the Lozi rose up against the Kololo in 1864 and forced them from power. Changed by their contact with the outsiders, the Lozi shifted their focus to raising cattle, building an army and exporting ivory. The military raided neighboring peoples and hunted elephants for their tusks, while the Lozi elite traded ivory for guns. This new way of life brought wealth to the aristocracy, but one-third of the population lived in poverty as serfs or slaves.

As Lozi society destabilized and Lunda and Ndongo declined in the 19th century, two empires arose to exploit the political and economic turmoil of west-central Africa. The Chokwe, originally hunters of the Angolan highlands, started an era of expansion to the north and west, into Lunda territory. Based in semiautonomous villages of up to 1,000 people, the Chokwe hunted ivory and gathered beeswax for trade with European merchants, who supplied them with firearms in exchange. During the 1870s, as the elephant population declined, the Chokwe began producing rubber for the rapidly expanding European market.

The Chokwe traded with foreigners via Ovimbundu merchants who lived to the east. As specialists in long-distance trade, the Ovimbundu sent huge caravans throughout the region, delivering imported goods to local peoples and collecting African products for sale to European traders on the Atlantic coast. The Ovimbundu prospered as the slave trade declined and the area's inhabitants turned their energies to producing other commodities, such as palm oil and rubber. But by the time the foreign demand for slaves began to fall, the slave trade had done irreparable damage to West African culture. Some societies had been ravaged by slave raids, while others had lost the ability to support themselves by means other than slaving. European involvement in the region had undermined traditional cultures. And rapid population growth in certain areas severely strained the area's resources. As if by design, European slavers had set the stage for colonialism in West Africa.

THE ORIGINAL
CITIZENS OF
SOUTHERN
AFRICA

Before Europeans set foot on the soil of southern Africa, that region was inhabited by many different peoples with diverse social, economic and political systems. Contrary to the assertions of Dutch and British colonizers, southern Africa was not an "empty" land waiting to be settled when white people arrived. Khoisan-speaking cultures had hunted and herded in the area for centuries before they were joined in medieval times by Bantu immigrants from the north, who imported agricultural ways. These groups developed cattle-centered economies in which wealth was accrued and power displayed through the possession of livestock. Chiefdoms based on cattle ownership emerged between 1100 and 1400, varying in size and organization depending on the demands of survival.

By 1500 almost every part of southern Africa (excluding the most forbidding desert areas) was occupied by organized societies, some more densely populated than others. When the Dutch decided to establish permanent settlements there in the 17th century, they simply

---

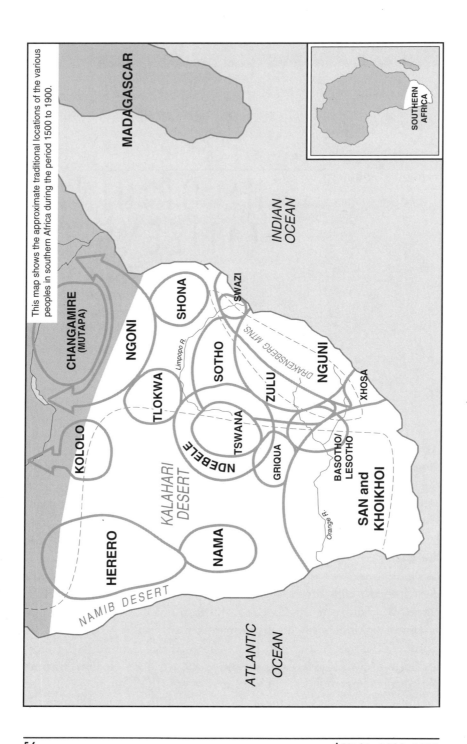

This map shows the approximate traditional locations of the various peoples in southern Africa during the period 1500 to 1900.

MADAGASCAR

SOUTHERN AFRICA

INDIAN OCEAN

CHANGAMIRE (MUTAPA)

NGONI

SHONA

SWAZI

KOLOLO

TLOKWA

SOTHO

Limpopo R.

DRAKENSBERG MTNS.

NGUNI

ZULU

XHOSA

NDEBELE

TSWANA

GRIQUA

BASOTHO/ LESOTHO

KALAHARI DESERT

HERERO

NAMA

Orange R.

SAN and KHOIKHOI

NAMIB DESERT

ATLANTIC OCEAN

evicted local people from their ancestral lands. The European push into southern Africa continued as white settlers demanded more land; Africans were forced into less hospitable territory or were subjugated to white rule. Pressure exerted by the white presence heightened internal and intergroup stresses among southern Africans, contributing to wars and political instability. Fighting ravaged local peoples during the 19th century, hastening the inexorable process of European colonization of southern Africa.

THE ARID WEST

Most of the western portion of southern Africa receives very little rainfall. Desert and near desert cover much of the area, although the region south of the Orange River is a bit wetter. Along the continent's southernmost coastline, around the Cape of Good Hope, the climate resembles that of the Mediterranean region, with more abundant vegetation and wildlife. The original inhabitants of Africa's extreme southwest adapted to the dryness, favoring nomadic pastoralism and hunting-gathering to agriculture as means of survival. These people, the San and the Khoikhoi, spoke Khoisan, a language characterized by a variety of clicking sounds. During Europe's Middle Ages, Bantu-speaking peoples arrived in the area and started farming on a small scale.

Living as nomads and moving from camp to camp as they exhausted local resources, the San were hunter-gatherers who traveled in small, isolated bands. They gathered berries and honey, harvested shellfish along coastal beaches, fished in rivers and hunted game in the interior. They traded some of their hunting produce to nearby farmers in exchange for copper, iron, tobacco and dagga, a form of marijuana. But because of their nomadic way of life, the San accumulated few possessions; the only animal they domesticated was the dog, which made a good hunting companion. Known as experts in the use of medicinal plants, the San were believed to command special magical powers. They also created beautiful artwork, despite the demands of their constant struggle for survival.

Also nomadic, the Khoikhoi herded cattle and sheep and stuck to the better-watered areas of southwestern Africa, where winter rainfall nourished the pastures their livestock required. Skilled at basketry,

An 18th-century engraving of a Khoikhoi encampment in southern Africa. (Picture Collection, The Branch Libraries, The New York Public Library)

weaving, pottery making and metal working, the Khoikhoi were organized into numerous small groups. They sold sheep and cattle to farming people in exchange for produce and items imported from the Indian Ocean coast, where Swahili and Portuguese merchants operated trading posts. Many of these items were brought to southwestern Africa by the Griqua, a Bantu people who hunted and traded across the Kalahari desert. To the north, in the grassy highlands between the Kalahari and the Namib desert, two other Bantu peoples—the Herero and the Nama—lived as nomadic pastoralists. Their competition for grazing land resulted in frequent warfare.

When Europeans first stopped at the Cape of Good Hope early in the 16th century, the Khoikhoi started a profitable trade in cattle and sheep. They sold their unwanted animals to the hungry seafarers, receiving metals, tobacco and beads in return. Before long, Dutch and Portuguese ships stopped regularly near the Cape to replenish their food stocks for the long voyage from Europe to Asia. The arrangement worked well as long as the Khoikhoi had extra livestock to sell. When increasingly frequent visitors began demanding more meat than the Khoikhoi wanted to provide, though, conflict resulted. The Dutch finally decided to stabilize their food supply by establishing a permanent settlement at Africa's southern tip, which they did in 1652. Their descendants came to be known first as Boers and later as Afrikaners.

As the Boer population grew and required more space, it gradually pushed local Africans off their land. For a while, the Khoikhoi managed to retain control of some land that could support them, but the San were squeezed into the desert. Some San assimilated into Khoikhoi groups, adopting pastoralist ways or hunting for the cattle herders. Others conducted cattle raids on Khoikhoi and Boer herds, an accepted African practice that angered the white settlers. In an effort to protect their livestock, the Boers slaughtered thousands of San during the 18th and 19th centuries, greatly reducing their numbers. The Boer expansion continued until few Khoikhoi or San remained in southwestern Africa.

THE FERTILE EAST

Bantu peoples who migrated into Khoikhoi and San territory during the 7th through 15th centuries sought to live where they could carry on their agricultural traditions. Scattered groups settled in the southwestern area, but the arid climate prohibited the development of extensive farming there. By contrast, the well-watered strip of land between the Drakensberg Mountains and the Indian Ocean was ideal for raising crops. Many Bantu immigrants settled there, forming the basis of the Nguni culture. Others settled on the wide grasslands, or high veld, west of the mountains, where they would evolve into the Sotho people. The new arrivals intermarried with the indigenous Khoikhoi and San, and on either side of the Drakensbergs new languages evolved that combined elements of Bantu and Khoisan. Migration in both directions across the mountains continued, and the Sotho and the Nguni remained linguistically as well as culturally related.

On the high veld, the Sotho, who included the Tswana, became great cattle herders. The limitations of the environment made interdependence between families a necessity, so the Sotho formed large political units centered around walled towns that housed up to several thousand people. As a source of food and a form of wealth, cattle were the foundation of Sotho culture. Cattle were used in every important social transaction—for instance, as part of the dowry paid by a man to the family of the woman he married. But the Sotho also hunted and engaged in agriculture, growing millet, sorghum, pumpkins and beans. Sotho artisans worked in metal and stone.

While the states formed by the southern Sotho never became highly centralized, the northern Sotho, and particularly the Tswana, built sophisticated bureaucracies. These states united smaller chiefdoms under a king called a *kgosi*, who left the minor rulers in place as long as they paid their annual tribute. The kgosi was a religious as well as political leader. One of his primary responsibilities was rain making, so periods of drought were viewed as signs that a kgosi's power was waning. The kgosi also oversaw the initiation of young people into adulthood and their division into age sets. Each age set had a distinct role in the community as workers or soldiers.

Based in capital towns of up to 20,000 residents, the kgosi supervised the administration of agriculture, which took place on fields surrounding the towns. They also watched over cattle herding operations farther afield and hunting in areas beyond the grazing lands. Each town was divided into wards containing clan units headed by a patriarch; each tributary chiefdom constituted a ward as well. Sotho states structured in this manner frequently underwent splits in which a patriarch or chief would migrate with his people and set up an independent chiefdom beyond the boundaries of the kgosi's kingdom. In this way the Sotho settled a large area west of the Drakensberg range with dozens of independent states.

View of the high veld and the Drakensberg Mountains in southern Africa. (Picture Collection, The Branch Libraries, The New York Public Library)

East of the Drakensbergs, meanwhile, the Nguni lived on self-sufficient homesteads, each of which was inhabited by a single kinship group. Centralization was unneccessary because the land yielded such plentiful crops that even small groups could support themselves easily. Homesteads that shared the same language and customs often united into loose chiefdoms, which in turn comprised several broad groupings of Nguni: the Xhosa, the Pondo, the Zulu, the Thembu and the Swazi. As farmers, herders, hunters and artisans the Nguni thrived, developing trade links with Zimbabwe and the Swahili city-states of the east coast via the Shona people to their north. The Zulu were particularly well known for their iron-smelting abilities, which they employed in the manufacture of fine weapons.

Indirect contact with European traders on the coast threw Nguni society into turmoil during the 18th century. When maize arrived in Africa from the Americas, the Nguni had a new crop that produced far larger yields than any of the traditional staples. The abundance of food led to population growth and an increase in the population density. As a result, more Nguni competed for land and fought over shrinking resources. Some groups struggled for control of the burgeoning trade in ivory for export to Europe, raiding their neighbors for access to elephant hunting grounds. One group, the Xhosa, expanded westward into Khoikhoi territory until they collided with Boers moving in from the opposite direction. The confrontation turned violent late in the 18th century. Indeed, as 1800 approached, the Nguni were wracked with political and military upheavals. Out of the disorder a new leader soon emerged.

SHAKA AND THE ZULU KINGDOM

In the early 19th century three main chiefdoms governed the northern Nguni: the Ngwane, led by a chief named Sobhuza; the Ndwandwe, led by Zwide; and the Mthethwa, led by Dingiswayo. The highly militarized states waged wars of expansion between 1800 and 1816, requiring all their young men to serve in the army and capturing cattle and soldiers from weaker chiefdoms. In 1816 a severe drought led to all-out war among the three major powers, which lasted three years. The Ndwandwe appeared to gain the upper hand against the Mthethwa in 1818, when Zwide captured and executed Dingiswayo, but the heir to Dingiswayo's military empire not only subdued the Ndwandwe but went on to conquer all the Nguni and many of the Sotho.

This leader was the Zulu chief named Shaka, who had served as one of Dingiswayo's regimental commanders. The illegitimate son of a Zulu chief, Shaka was born in 1787. Knowing his future among the Zulu held little promise, as a teenager he left home for Dingiswayo's court. Shaka became a favorite of the Mthethwa king and rose through the military ranks. When Shaka's father died in 1816, Dingiswayo ousted the rightful heir to the throne and installed Shaka as chief of the Zulu. Respected as a brilliant military strategist and feared as a ferocious warrior, Shaka easily assumed control of Dingiswayo's empire when his mentor was killed.

Shaka immediately set about refining Dingiswayo's military system. He required all male members of certain age sets to serve as soldiers and forbad them to marry until they had completed their military service at age 40. He introduced hand-to-hand combat with the sharp stabbing spear called the *assagai*, making his forces far more lethal than those that relied on the traditional throwing spear. Requiring his army, or *impi,* to go barefoot for greater mobility (they had previously worn sandals), Shaka drilled his men in orderly regiments that could charge an enemy more effectively than could the disorganized mob used in most Nguni battles. He perfected techniques of espionage, of surrounding the enemy and of launching sneak attacks. His guiding military tactic was to destroy his enemies rather than to subdue them.

With this formidable force of highly trained and disciplined impi Shaka set out to expand his kingdom, which he called Zulu. He forced the Ndwandwe to flee northward into Changamire territory, where they became known as the Ngoni and began raiding East African peoples. The Ngwane were also pushed north out of Nguni territory; they settled along the lower Limpopo River and eventually formed the Swazi state in the 1830s, after Shaka's death. If they submitted quickly and humbly, Shaka absorbed the peoples he conquered into the Zulu kingdom, although he always killed their royalty. He added the young men of these societies to his army, where they quickly became loyal to him. Living, working and fighting together in regiments that incorporated soldiers from various Nguni groups, Shaka's impi soon identified themselves as Zulus, no matter where they came from. And because most able-bodied men belonged to Zulu regiments, local leaders could never build opposition forces with which to resist Shaka.

In only a few years Shaka commanded a force of 50,000 soldiers and controlled 15,000 square miles of territory in southeast Africa. He built a highly centralized government in which he held absolute authority as king. Royal appointees governed outlying provinces, monitored by Shaka's female relatives, while the impi established regimental towns at strategic locations to maintain Shaka's control over all his territory. Young women as well as young men were formed into regiments that fulfilled such functions as farming and also fought when neccessary. The state controlled food production, diverting as much as needed to feed the large standing army. Shaka himself oversaw religious activity, outlawing regional variations in order to enforce a measure of cultural unity among those whom he conquered. To encourage dedication to the Zulu kingdom, loyal subjects were amply rewarded and disloyal ones severely punished.

To keep his empire afloat, Shaka had to maintain a constant state of war, in which his impi continually conquered and looted other peoples. As fewer states remained to be conquered, and as those that did learned to defend themselves against the Zulu, it was increasingly difficult for Shaka to support his army and control his people. But Shaka did not live to see his empire fall. In 1828 two of his half-brothers assassinated him; one took over the throne after murdering the other. Without Shaka's leadership, the Zulu kingdom's period of glory came to an end. It was surrounded by enemies, for Shaka had made no friends. When the Boers started invading Zulu territory, the weakened kingdom had no allies to assist in its defense.

MFECANE/DIFAQANE

Forty years of war in Nguni and Sotho country forced thousands upon thousands of refugees to flee their homes. Starting during the time of war between the Ngwane, the Ndwandwe and the Mthethwa, the stream of refugees turned into a flood during Shaka's brutal 10-year reign. The upheaval did not stop until about 1840, by which time the map of southeastern Africa had been completely redrawn. The Nguni called this period the Mfecane, or the crushing; the Sotho, into whose territory many Nguni fled, called it the Difaqane, or the scattering.

Refugees from the northern Nguni wars scattered in all directions, leaving vast areas completely depopulated. But rather than settling peacefully elsewhere, most of the refugees formed bands that adopted Zulu military techniques. They invaded the new territory, attacking the peoples who lived there and looting their herds of cattle. The small chiefdoms of the southern Nguni and the Sotho made easy prey for the raiders, and entire villages were wiped out. Peoples lucky enough to escape direct attack fled before the wave of Nguni invaders, often seeking refuge in hilly country.

Both the southern Nguni refugees and those they terrorized established states whose chief purpose was to defend against assaults by Zulu impi or other enemies. Between 1820 and 1850 dozens of new chiefdoms appeared on the high veld and at the southern and northern extremes of the Zulu empire. One such state was Swazi, formed by Ngwane, who chose not to submit to Shaka's rule. Another was Ndebele, which encompassed the land occupied by the Tswana. Vio-

MOSHOESHOE

When Nguni refugees started invading Sotho territory in the 1810s, Moshoeshoe was a Sotho chief with several thousand subjects. By 1821 he recognized the need for better protection against the refugees' attacks and looting, and he moved with his people to a flat-topped mountain in a region less prone to attack. He set up a fortress on the mountaintop, overlooking the grazing lands where his people lived. Whenever attackers approached, Moshoeshoe's people took refuge in the fortress while his soldiers rolled boulders down the mountainside to crush their opponents.

Moshoeshoe's success in defending his people led nearby chiefs to seek his protection. These chiefdoms formed a confederacy under Moshoeshoe's leadership, which came to be known as the kingdom of Basotho. By 1833 he ruled about 25,000 subjects, a number that grew to 80,000 by 1848. Moshoeshoe held title to all the kingdom's cattle, lending the livestock to his subjects for their use. To broaden his influence and cement ties with susidiary chiefs, he took many wives and established his relatives in positions of responsibility. He let the groups under his control carry on their own customs and traditions, thereby earning their respect and loyalty.

Moshoeshoe bolstered the security of his kingdom by paying tribute to potential aggressors, such as the Zulu and the Ndebele. He also cultivated friendly relations with white settlers, winning their trust by inviting Christian missionaries onto his land. Moshoeshoe had no intention of converting to Christianity, and few of his people did so, but he did acquire guns and horses, thus strengthening his military position. By avoiding war whenever possible, he grew stronger as other states exhausted their resources in wars. Cattle raids by his people against Boer herds brought Moshoeshoe into conflict with one group of whites, but he developed good relations with the growing numbers of British in southern Africa. In 1843 Moshoeshoe signed a treaty with the British that brought Basotho under the crown's protection. The move reduced his own authority but saved his people from complete subjugation.

lent Ndebele raiders built a powerful kingdom on the high veld before being expelled from the area by Zulu, Griqua and Boer forces. Another people forced off the high veld were the Kololo, who moved into Lozi territory on the Zambezi River floodplains.

The Kololo left the high veld under attack from the Batlokwa, or Tlokwa, people. Ruled by a woman named Mantatisi, who was regent for her young son Senkonyela, the Tlokwa became warriors in their own defense after they were set upon by bands of refugees from the Zulu wars. Mantatisi moved her people to a mountaintop for protection and started raiding neighbors, such as the Kololo, seeking to expand Tlokwa holdings. Once Senkonyela took over as chief, the Tlokwa directed their military energies toward the Basotho to their south.

The Basotho, also based on a mountaintop in the high veld, were led by a chief named Moshoeshoe, whose diplomatic skill and desire for peace allowed his people to outlast the chaos of the Mfecane/Difaqane. He resisted the excesses of war and concentrated on establishing a stable state. Moshoeshoe laid the foundations of the modern state of Lesotho, one of the few areas to maintain some degree of autonomy during the colonial era. Their energies depleted by constant war, most of the other peoples of the region were crushed by white colonizers during the 19th century.

EUROPEAN TRADE AND INFLUENCE TO 1650

By 1500 Europeans had explored the Atlantic and Indian Ocean coasts of Africa and had established their first outposts on the continent. Europeans were interested in Africa primarily for profit: By learning about its shoreline, they hoped to chart a sea route to India. Such a route would allow them to divert the lucrative trade in exotic Asian goods away from the Muslims of Arabia and North Africa, who had monopolized it up to then. Along the way, European explorers planned to make contact with African kingdoms and start trading with them. Renaissance Europeans knew almost nothing about Africa, but they had long heard rumors of gold-rich empires south of the Sahara.

A secondary motivation for European exploration of Africa's perimeter was a desire to vanquish the Muslim "infidels" who ruled the northern third of the continent. The Moors—as Europeans called the dark-skinned Muslims—had invaded Christian Europe during the age of Islamic expansion and had been pushed back into North Africa only during the last century. Many Europeans wanted to extinguish the "evil" of Islam altogether; they saw Africa as the logical starting place for their "holy war." They had heard of the Christian kingdom of Ethiopia and thought an alliance with that nation would help them in their cause, but they did not know where it was. Some held out hope that all of sub-Saharan Africa—not just Ethiopia—was Christian.

The Portuguese were the first Europeans with the shipbuilding and navigational skills to launch expeditions along Africa's Atlantic coast. They found the Gold Coast (the coast of modern Ghana) in 1471, rounded the Cape of Good Hope in 1488 and visited Ethiopia for the first time in 1490. After establishing forts to protect their interests, the Portuguese began sending annual trading fleets to Africa and India in 1499. The pace of trade soon picked up. Ocean shipping proved a much quicker way to bring African and Asian goods to Europe than the traditional system of trans-Saharan caravans and Mediterranean galleys. As the long-distance sea routes supplanted the old trading networks, the Portuguese earned enormous profits. They all but eliminated would-be Italian, Spanish, French and British competitors from the African arena. After Christopher Columbus' 1492 voyage west across the Atlantic, the rest of Europe turned its attention to the Americas. For several decades the Portuguese had little competition for trade with Africa.

Concentrating on the east coast, where the Swahili city-states already formed a sophisticated mercantile network, and on the west coast between the Sahara and the Namib deserts, Portuguese traders sought to tap into Africa's existing trading systems. Because their chief interests lay with India, at first they viewed Africa as a stopover rather than a destination, a place where they could pick up whatever extra profits came easily. They did not, for the most part, attempt to develop new forms of trade with Africa. Instead, the Portuguese purchased gold, ivory, wrought iron, tortoiseshell, textiles and other items that were readily available.

African rulers maintained authority over the trade with the foreigners, even where the Europeans raided cities or set up fortresses. The Portuguese, in turn, respected the power and sophistication of their African trading partners and relied on diplomacy rather than force to further their ends—at least initially. But the European arrival in Africa coincided with a period of internal political instability there. The Portuguese soon forgot their original courtesy and reaped even larger profits by taking advantage of African wars and intrigue.

THE PORTUGUESE IN WEST AFRICA

Until the mid-1600s, Europeans were most interested in Africa as a source of a single commodity: gold. As a result, Portuguese explorers focused their early efforts on finding the Gold Coast. When they did, its wealth surpassed their wildest expectations, and they dubbed the area *el mina* (the mine). The Portuguese built their first African fort, São Jorge de Mina, there in 1482; the city that grew up around it came to be known as Elmina. Three more forts soon appeared nearby. In the early days, relations between the Africans and the Portuguese on the Gold Coast were peaceful, for the local kings permitted the newcomers to build their forts in exchange for a promise to pay annual tribute. The gold mines remained under African jurisdiction, and the foreigners participated in the gold trade only to the extent they were allowed to do so. Many of the area's chiefs negotiated alliances with the Portuguese, whose forts and ships regulated naval trade.

In exchange for the quantities of gold they shipped back to Portugal, the Portuguese imported cloth, metal, beads and slaves to the Gold Coast. Most of these items they purchased elsewhere along the coast, where African merchants came from the interior to trade with them. During the late 15th and early 16th centuries the leading non-gold-trading partner of the Portuguese was Benin. Benin's wars of expansion yielded it a surplus of captives, which the Portuguese bought to resell to the mining operators of the Gold Coast. When the wars ended in 1516 Benin had fewer slaves to sell but still supplied pepper, ivory, natural gums and cloth purchased from Yoruba peoples of the interior. Benin's reluctance to provide as many slaves as the Portuguese wanted, and Portuguese reluctance to provide Benin with firearms, ultimately led to conflict between the trading partners. The Portuguese left Benin for more profitable territory about 1520.

As trading communities took shape around the new forts of the Gold Coast, the Portuguese governed activity in these towns according to their own rules. The most significant authority they asserted was to punish African merchants who traded with the non-Portuguese ships that sailed the coast in growing numbers as the 16th century progressed. In retaliation, Africans could withhold food and water, which the Portuguese could not supply for themselves. The tensions became more serious in the second half of the century, as Portuguese strength and numbers increased and as they tried to claim greater control of the gold trade. In 1576 local African rulers issued a warning by destroying the Portuguese fort at Accra. The threat worked; the Portuguese were held in check for the remainder of their stay on the Gold Coast.

Southeast of the Gold Coast, the Portuguese made one of the few serious European efforts at colonizing African soil. Unlike the Americas, which were sparsely populated and had climates agreeable to Europeans, densely populated tropical Africa presented fewer opportunities for white settlement. But São Tomé and Príncipe, two fertile, uninhabited islands convenient to passing ships, offered ideal locations for Portuguese settlement. The Portuguese set up plantations that became Europe's main source of sugar during the 1500s. Large numbers of slaves, brought from the mainland, worked the plantations. Between 1500 and 1575, the Portuguese imported about 1,000 slaves annually to work on São Tomé and Príncipe.

Across the Atlantic Ocean, meanwhile, Portuguese colonizers established plantations in Brazil and other Europeans set up a few estates on the islands of the Caribbean Sea. The Portuguese of São Tomé and Príncipe shipped the first African slaves to the New World in 1532. During the 1530s these islands became the principle location from which slaves were sent to the Americas. The numbers were slow but steady until the middle of the 1600s, when the New World plantation economy and the accompanying slave trade mushroomed. By that time the sugar plantations of São Tomé and Príncipe had fallen victim to competition from the booming sugar industry of the Americas.

The kingdom of Kongo was one source of slaves bought by the Portuguese for export. Impressed with the large, highly organized state, the Portuguese established diplomatic and trade ties with the kingdom in the 1480s. The newcomers saw Kongo as a source of copper, salt, cloth and slaves, while the Kongolese saw the foreigners as a source of education, training and guns. At the invitation of the king, the Portuguese sent missionaries and artisans to the region to help Kongo in its various reform efforts. In 1506 a Kongolese convert to Christianity seized the throne and crowned himself Afonso I. Afonso started corresponding with the king of Portugal and the Roman Catholic pope, who at first dealt with him as an equal. To counter resistance to his rule, Afonso employed Portuguese weapons and soldiers, consolidating power in his hands. His methods sparked rebellions and plunged Kongo into a period of civil war.

By this time the Portuguese had come to view Kongo mainly as a source of slaves. The constant warfare under Afonso's rule provided a steady stream of captives for sale, so the Portuguese encouraged the king's enemies in their uprisings. Amid the chaos, many Kongolese entered the lucrative slave trade and in turn stirred up the kind of trouble that increased the supply of slaves. The Portuguese demanded more and more slaves as Kongo grew weaker and more unstable. Afonso's successors tried to expel the Portuguese and then, when they failed, attempted to take control of the slave trade. At the same time, the Portuguese began buying captives from the neighboring Ndongo and promoted war between Kongo and Ndongo to keep the slave supply steady. Kongo was conquered by the invading Jaga in 1568, then restored in 1574 by the Portuguese, who installed a puppet king. But warfare and slaving continued to take a toll, and Kongo disintegrated early in the 17th century.

The Portuguese turned increasing attention to Ndongo, where rumors of silver in the mountains led them to attempt direct colonization. After setting up a base at Luanda in 1575, they invaded the interior in the 1580s. They met strong resistance, however, and soon gave up their plan. But they found that ongoing local wars provided them with plenty of captive slaves, which they bought in exchange for firearms and rum—two products that further destabilized the area. Well into the 17th century, fighting throughout the area now occupied by Angola kept the Portuguese well supplied with slaves for export to their colony in Brazil. The disruptions also kept the local states vulnerable to eventual colonization.

THE PORTUGUESE IN EAST AFRICA

Once the Portuguese rounded the southern tip of Africa and found their way north and east across the Indian Ocean to India, they determined to set up bases along Africa's east coast. These bases were to serve as launching points for trade with Asia and sites for contact with local African traders. Starting about 1505, the Portuguese systematically took over naval trade along the East African coast by seizing the Swahili city-states that flourished there. The technique involved threatening each city with invasion and looting unless the local ruler agreed

ETHIOPIA

Engraving of the Ethiopian court receiving Portuguese missionaries in the 16th century. (Picture Collection, The Branch Libraries, The New York Public Library)

European hopes of gaining a foothold in Africa by forming an alliance with the Christian kingdom of Ethiopia met with bitter disappointment. When the Portuguese became the first modern Europeans to visit Ethiopia, in 1490, they found an empire in decline. Internal power struggles and assaults from Muslim enemies had weakened the kingdom, leaving it in no position to help the Europeans "Christianize" Africa. And although they were cordial to their visiting fellow Christians, the Ethiopians shared little religious common ground with them. While the Portuguese adhered to Roman Catholicism, the

to accept the Portuguese presence and submit to Portuguese authority. Because the 40-odd cities were more accustomed to competing rather than cooperating with each other, they were vulnerable to Portuguese force. Two—Malindi and Zanzibar—surrendered without a struggle, but the others resisted and were sacked. The Portuguese justified the violence as "holy war" against the Muslim populations.

By 1510 the Portuguese took command of all the trading cities of East Africa's southern coast. Despite efforts by Egypt and Ottoman

Ethiopians practiced the ancient Monophysite version of Coptic Christianity, which was considered heretical in Europe. Aside from a belief in Jesus Christ, few Ethiopian concerns or interests coincided with those of the Portuguese.

Cautious about the strangers who arrived on their shores in 1490, the Ethiopians did not allow their Portuguese visitors to leave the country. The Portuguese next sent envoys in 1510, who were also forbidden to leave. Another mission, sent in 1520, was finally allowed to return to Portugal in 1526 and make a report to the king and to the pope. The Ethiopians did not invite further contact with the Portuguese for another 15 years. During the intervening period, Muslims from nearby Adal launched a series of attacks against the kingdom. When Ethiopia felt severely threatened by growing Muslim military power, it enlisted Portuguese aid, and in 1543 a small force of Portuguese expelled the Muslims from Ethiopian territory.

Many of the Portuguese soldiers stayed on in Ethiopia, joined by Jesuit missionaries who went to convert the local people to Catholicism. The Ethiopians received modern firearms and military training from the Portuguese, some of whom built lavish castles near Lake Tana. In 1622 King Susenyos converted to Catholicism, and the Portuguese believed their future in Ethiopia was secured. But the Ethiopian population resented the accelerated activities of the missionaries, and in 1648 they expelled the Jesuits. For the next 200 years Ethiopia banned all foreign missionaries and isolated itself from the rest of the world.

Turkey to force them out of the Indian Ocean, the Portuguese established themselves firmly in the region, with Mozambique as their headquarters. They built stone fortresses in Kilwa, Sofala and Mozambique and put down periodic uprisings along the northern coast. Mombasa, the city most resistant to Portuguese rule, was sacked in 1505, 1528 and 1589 and finally brought under control in 1599, when the Portuguese erected the mammoth Fort Jesus and made the city their new headquarters.

As on the west coast, gold was the East African export that most interested the Portuguese in the 16th century. Despite their strong presence in the region, however, they did not monopolize trade there. They collected tribute from the Swahili traders but exerted little political influence over their activities. The Europeans did not, at first, venture inland or try to develop new avenues of commerce; they merely attached themselves to the existing system. But the Portuguese presence did disrupt traditional trading patterns. Swahili traders resentful of the foreign intrusion diverted the flow of gold and other items away from the cities occupied by the Portuguese and toward posts farther south.

Frustrated by the Swahili move, the Portuguese pushed up the Zambezi River into the interior in the 1530s. They raided the trading posts the Swahili had set up along the river and tried to take over gold mining and trading activities there. Enjoying only partial success, the Portuguese attempted to achieve political dominance over the local Mutapa people by converting them to Christianity and joining with them against the Swahili Muslims. Portuguese settlers known as prazeros married into the local royalty and established plantations called prazos while Dominican and Jesuit missionaries went to work. But their plan didn't succeed, for the Portuguese enslaved some local people, taxed others heavily and alienated all.

The Portuguese next launched an all-out military campaign in the 1560s and early 1570s, struggling to establish their authority in the interior, but fierce resistance and deadly tropical diseases defeated them. After another failed assault in 1574, the Portuguese made a treaty with the Mutapa king against the Swahili. Neither the Mutapa nor the Portuguese were ever strong enough to control the gold trade, however, and the treaty proved useless. In the early decades of the 17th century the East African ports declined in importance as other European navigators found quicker routes to India farther out to sea. Portuguese hopes for East Africa were dashed.

THE END OF PORTUGUESE DOMINANCE

The profits made by the Portuguese in Africa eventually attracted the attention of other Europeans despite the distractions presented by the Americas. Independent explorations of sea routes around Africa brought the French around the Cape of Good Hope in 1529, the

English in 1580 and the Dutch in 1595. These three powers immediately started competing with Portugal for African, Indian and Asian trade. Britain founded its East India Company in 1600, the Netherlands launched its equivalent operation two years later and France started its own version in 1664. The purpose of these companies was to develop the spice trade with India. Except as a source of slaves for New World plantations, Africa was primarily a port of call.

As the English, French and Dutch started dispatching regular fleets to trade in East Africa and across the Indian Ocean, the Portuguese monopoly in the region collapsed. By 1610 the Dutch were the chief power in the Indian Ocean. Setting up bases on the island of Mauritius, east of Madagascar, and on the Cape of Good Hope, the Dutch bypassed the East African coast on their way to Asia. The British and French established a growing presence there as Portuguese power waned and as ivory and slaves replaced gold as the chief exports. Their interest in the area was strictly commercial, so they stayed out of the way as the Omani Arabs took over local rule between 1650 and 1698. Late in the 1600s the Mutapa joined with the Changamire to drive the Portuguese out of the interior; the last Portuguese were expelled from Mombasa 1698.

On the west coast, the Dutch West India Company took over the Portuguese posts between 1637 and 1642. From this point on, the vast majority of European trade with Africa occurred on the stretch of Atlantic shoreline between the Senegal and Congo rivers. Until 1650 the Europeans focused on the gold trade. Their activities, like those of the Portuguese, were extremely limited and had little impact on Africans in the continent's interior. Long stretches of coastline were ignored, but in those areas visited by the Europeans, sub-Saharan Africans became more aware of the wider world. They acquired new crops, new tools and new skills and joined the international trading community. But the outcome of European contact was to be far from beneficial for most Africans. After about 1650, the main African export became slaves, whom the Europeans exported to their rapidly growing plantations in the New World. The slave trade would leave many African societies in ruins.

THE SLAVE TRADE, 1650–1880

The commerce in African slaves might have remained only a small part of the continent's trade with the outside world were it not for the 17th-century plantation boom in the Americas and the Caribbean islands. As the Spanish, British, Dutch, French, Portuguese, Danish and other Europeans rushed to claim a piece of the New World, they established large plantations and mines on abundant, sparsely populated land that seemed free for the taking. There they grew tobacco, coffee, indigo, cotton and sugarcane for eager consumers back home and extracted silver and gold to enrich their national treasuries. Each of these enterprises required large amounts of labor; plantation and mine owners sought to maximize their profits by exploiting the unpaid labor of slaves.

At first, the Europeans tried enslaving the indigenous American and Caribbean populations, but these "Indians," as they were mistakenly called, soon died of diseases imported by the colonizers. Plantation and mine operators next turned to forced labor supplied by criminals and indentured servants sent from Europe. Their demand for labor, however, far outstripped the supply of white workers, so they looked to

Africa, from which the Portuguese had exported small numbers of slaves since early in the 16th century. Tapping established trade networks, Europeans soon found they could obtain all the slaves they wanted from the shores of West Africa. The trade in human cargo quickly overshadowed all other forms of commerce between Europe and Africa; for more than 200 years it was a key component of the Western world's economic system.

Slavery, of course, was nothing new to the Africans. Like much of Europe in the Middle Ages, many African societies had a feudal structure, in which kings were served by vassals, or nobles, who in turn were served by the mass of the kingdom's subjects. In this system, people owed service to those above them in the social hierarchy. The lowest-ranked Africans could be compared to European serfs, who as near slaves had no choice but to work for their masters. Certain criminals, outcasts and prisoners of war enjoyed no freedoms at all and lived in bondage.

But, in contrast to the people sold to Europeans for export, African serfs and slaves remained recognized members of society. Unlike those who were shipped to the plantations and mines of the New World, they were viewed as productive individuals rather than as livestock, real estate or other property. Low-ranking subjects could rise in the hierarchy and slaves could earn their freedom. Born into the cultures they served or captured by people similar to them, African slaves were not considered inferior to their masters in anything other than a social sense. They were accorded basic respect as humans.

Africa had also exported slaves for centuries. Since ancient times, the Muslims of North Africa had imported black Africans from across the Sahara for the elite citizens of Morocco, Algeria, Tunis, Tripoli and Egypt. They exported a few of these slaves to Europe and greater numbers to Turkey and the Middle East. Elsewhere, the Swahili traders of the east coast had long sold slaves to Arab merchants who plied the Indian Ocean and the Red Sea. These slaves went to Arabia, Persia (Iran), India and perhaps China.

But, unlike the mostly male captives exported for hard physical labor in the New World, two-thirds of the slaves traded via trans-Saharan and Indian Ocean routes before 1800 were women. Many of these women were sold as concubines. Whatever their gender, virtually all the slaves were destined for service in wealthy households. Until the

19th century the numbers of Africans sold via these routes were very small, amounting to no more than a few thousand people annually.

Starting about 1650, Europeans introduced a new kind of slavery to Africa, focusing their activities on the west coast between modern-day Senegal and Angola. Desperate for unpaid workers to perform the harsh duties of mining and plantation farming, the Europeans bought as many African captives as local rulers would sell. They handled these slaves as livestock, stripping them naked for inspections and packing them into crowded ships. Africans entered the trade for the big profits they could make in firearms and other European goods. When the foreign slavers demanded more captives, African traders scrambled to supply them for fear of losing out to neighbors competing for good relations with the Europeans. The Europeans demanded huge numbers of slaves—tens of thousands annually. Before long, the West African economy revolved around a single commodity: slaves.

THE FOREIGN SLAVERS

The Spanish colonies in the Americas and the Caribbean obtained African slaves from Portuguese naval traders as early as the 1530s. Based on Africa's Atlantic coast, these traders supplied slaves to the Portuguese colony of Brazil as well. At first, only a few thousand Africans were shipped to the New World each year, but as the number of plantations and mines there grew, the flow of slaves increased. By 1600 about 275,000 Africans had been exported from West Africa. The pace picked up in the 17th century, a period of rapid European exploration and expansion, especially in the Americas. Several countries—Britain, France, the Netherlands and Denmark among them—gained the naval technology that had taken Spain and Portugal across the Atlantic. They established their own colonies and began to capitalize on the rich resources of the New World.

At the same time, these nations sailed into African waters that up to then had been controlled by the Portuguese. They needed slaves to work in their colonies, and the Portuguese had demonstrated that Africa could supply those slaves. Slowly but surely, the Portuguese lost their grip on the West African coast. The superior naval, military and mercantile abilities of their competitors spelled the end of their monopoly on trade with Africa. Between 1637 and 1642 the Dutch seized the Portuguese forts along the Gold Coast and established themselves as the dominant power in the area. The Dutch West India Company launched high-volume slave trading with the European colonies in the Caribbean and the Americas.

From 1642 to about 1700 the Dutch commanded most of the African slave trade, pioneering the techniques, customs and routes of the lucrative business. Expanding the trading networks established by the Portuguese and feeding the existing African taste for European goods, they built a massive industry. They supplied slaves not only to Dutch colonies in the New World but to the British and French there as well. (The British had forced the Spanish out of North America and the Caribbean by then.) Concerned that the Dutch controlled such a vital element of colonial enterprise, the British and French began to make inroads into the Dutch trade. Commercial competition and military confrontation between European opponents made the slave trade in Africa especially violent between 1650 and 1700.

The efforts of French and British traders gained momentum from a series of wars between the Netherlands, England and France that racked Europe between 1652 and 1713. These wars seriously compromised the strength of the Netherlands. Around 1700, Britain and France assumed leadership of the African slave trade, the British controlling the Gold Coast and areas to the east, the French dominating the region south of the Senegal River. In the area now known as Angola the Portuguese retained a foothold, exporting slaves to Brazil. All told, between 1600 and 1700 more than 1.3 million Africans were kidnapped and sent across the Atlantic.

Until the 18th century the slave trade was conducted by a few large companies, such as the Dutch West India Company, officially chartered and controlled by the governments of the slaving European nations. As demand for slaves skyrocketed beyond the capacity of these state monopolies, European governments opened the trade to everyone. The 18th century was the period of peak activity in the African slave trade, when up to 100,000 people a year were sold into bondage— a total of more than 6 million between 1700 and 1800. In the free market the British gradually outpaced their competitors, reigning as leader between 1750 and 1800. At times they were responsible for half or more of the total number of people bought and sold.

The African slave trade was but one leg of the "triangular trade" that developed between Europe, Africa and the New World. Under this system, the first leg of the triangle involved the sale of European manufactured goods to Africans in exchange for slaves. Although this was the least profitable portion of the triangular trade, income from the export was quite impressive: In the late 1700s Europe exported an estimated £2 million ($10 million) of goods to Africa annually. There, the second and more profitable leg of the triangle originated: the sale of African slaves to plantation and mine owners in the Americas and the Caribbean. Because of the risks inherent in this segment of the triangular trade, European merchants viewed it as subsidiary to the most profitable activity of all: the third leg, along which slave-grown New World produce was shipped to the European market. Cotton, rum, coffee, tobacco and other products commanded high prices in Europe, but the biggest import of all was sugar. In 1720 New World plantations shipped half a million tons of sugar to England alone; by the end of the century the annual figure was five times greater.

Thus, slaving was a key element of an immensely profitable trading system. Without slaves, European colonizers could not have exploited New World resources so efficiently. Until the 19th century, however, plantation and mine operators' use of slaves was far from efficient. They worked the slaves so hard and treated them so badly that few Africans survived longer than 10 years in the Americas and the Caribbean. Few slave owners cared to replenish their supply of slaves through natural means, for childbearing removed mothers from the workforce and produced new slaves only after many years of feeding and clothing slave children. As a result, European slavers worked to meet a constantly high demand for new captives from Africa.

They fulfilled this task from bases on the coast of Africa, rarely venturing into the interior. African traders, who most often worked for African kings, brought people to the European outposts for sale. These captives were usually prisoners of war. Fearing retribution from African rulers, Europeans seldom kidnapped Africans themselves. On those rare occasions when they did, it was usually intended as a warning to unhappy African trading partners that the foreigners intended to obtain slaves by any means necessary. But for the most part the European slave traders kept to the coast, where they maintained the

Engraving of slaves being marched to market on the African coast. (Picture Collection, The Branch Libraries, The New York Public Library)

flow of slaves by encouraging Africans in wars against each other. Sometimes they sent their African servants or slaves on trading missions to interior kingdoms; the Portuguese in Angola called these agents *pombieros*.

On the coast the European slavers subjected the people brought to them for sale to degrading physical examinations. Having survived a long, cruel march to the coast, men, women and children alike were handled like cattle and stripped naked for inspection. Anyone deemed to be ill, weak, less than 12 years old or over the age of 35 was rejected as unfit and returned to the African traders. Those whom the slavers purchased were branded with the shipping company's mark and crowded into holding pens to await their fate. The humiliating dehumanization involved in the process weakened the resistance of many of the victims, making them less likely to rebel and escape. Once loaded on board ship, they would endure a long voyage in cramped, filthy conditions before reaching their destination. On average, one in eight—and often many more—would die at sea. Those who dared to fight their captors would be harshly punished or even killed.

Motivated by the large profits to be made in Africa, European slave traders ignored the horrors associated with the slave trade. They came to regard Africans as less human than themselves and even viewed slavery as beneficial to the "savages." Slavery, they claimed, exerted a "civilizing" influence on the "barbaric" Africans and "rescued" them from lives of misery. At the same time, many considered the slave trade a noble crusade to spread Christianity to the "Dark Continent." The European attitudes born during the era of the slave trade would in time fuel the European conquest of Africa.

THE IMPACT ON AFRICANS

Despite European assertions to the contrary, the slave trade was enormously destructive to African culture. A small number of African kings and merchants grew rich and powerful as the result of the slave trade, but their gains were temporary. Meanwhile, lasting harm was done to the economies of slaving regions, and millions of Africans suffered as a result. The gap between rich and poor people widened, while rulers involved in the slave trade neglected long-term economic planning in other areas, such as agriculture and industry. In addition, the loss of 12 to 15 million strong, productive people to the Atlantic slave trade in less than 400 years hit the economy hard. Workers who would have contributed to African growth were torn from their homes and their labor exploited to enrich Europe and the Americas.

The slave trade did not affect every area of Africa. Most of the people shipped across the Atlantic came from the coastal areas between Senegal and Angola; the intensity of activity along the shoreline of present-day Nigeria prompted Europeans to term that region the Slave Coast. After 1800, slaving along the east coast picked up, concentrating in the area now occupied by Mozambique and Tanzania. The direct impact of the slave trade did not extend more than perhaps 200 miles inland, but its repercussions rippled through the entire continent. Every society within striking distance of the coast lost people to slavery. Among those hardest hit were the Mandinka, Yoruba, Tukolor, Fulani, Kongo and Ndongo of the west coast and the Xhosa of the east coast.

Local kings controlled the African side of the slave trade. Many entered the trade reluctantly, realizing if they didn't they might fall victim to slave raids by neighboring peoples. As guns arrived on the scene and a few kings started using them against each other, African rulers knew they had to purchase the new weapons in order to protect their people. For most, the only way to buy guns, ammunition and replacement parts was with slaves. The great wealth to be gained through commerce with the Europeans also drew Africans into the trade. Only by trafficking in slaves could they so easily obtain such large quantities of textiles, iron, copper, metalwares, cowrie shells and other valuable goods. If they were to safeguard the security and prosperity of their kingdoms, most rulers in slaving regions found they had little choice but to enter the slave trade.

Africans did, however, retain a good deal of control over the slave trade. They charged rent on land occupied by European slaving centers and permitted Europeans to operate only if they recognized African sovereignty and agreed to pay taxes or tribute on their profits. At least initially, African kings sold only as many slaves as were readily available. Most of the people they sold were captives taken during wars of expansion and conquest; few of these wars were fought solely for the purpose of capturing slaves. Kings rarely sold their own people, except those considered outcasts, criminals, insane or ill. When they made sales to the slavers they drove hard bargains, accepting only those agreements they deemed sufficiently profitable.

The rapid influx of wealth and firearms into West Africa allowed some rulers to build large, powerful states. Slave-trading kings used their new weapons in wars that extended their influence and consolidated smaller chiefdoms into unified empires. Especially along the Slave Coast, towns that served as slaving centers grew rich and powerful, sometimes establishing themselves as independent city-states. Some states started using slaves in large numbers for agriculture and mining, further adding to royal wealth. A class of merchant-princes emerged; these were traders who used their business skills and clan links to build large trading empires that cultivated close connections with the Europeans.

The changing political landscape led to turmoil as conflicts developed between traditional rulers and merchant-princes, between old states and new states and between longtime neighbors. Rival states struggled to control trade with the Europeans and funnel slaving profits into their own treasuries. Some old states fell and new empires arose in the chaos ushered in by the slave trade; certain smaller cultures were completely wiped out or sold into slavery. The almost unbroken state of war in the slaving regions created a steady supply of prisoners to be sold to the Europeans. Profiting from the internal upheavals in African society, the Europeans continued to supply guns to all takers. They formed informal alliances with rival kings, bringing the African rulers into their sphere of influence while making no genuine effort to assist them or to promote peace.

The political devastation wrought on Africa by the slave trade made the economic consequences of slaving even worse than they might otherwise have been. In pursuit of profits, some rulers abused their power and ignored the possible consequences of their actions. Constant warfare shifted attention away from the agricultural and crafts activities that helped build a strong economy. Political crisis forced leaders to make decisions based on short-range rather than long-range needs. Fighting and slave raids disrupted normal agricultural and trading patterns. Governed by uncertainty and fear, many Africans saw the slave trade as their only means of survival.

By the 18th century, the slave trade overwhelmed the West African economy. The import of manufactured goods from Europe slowed the development of local industries and made Africans dependent on Europe for certain basic items. In exchange for these goods, Europeans sought a single commodity, slaves, in greater quantities each year. Because slaving removed millions of productive workers from Africa without replacing them with any goods or technology of lasting value, it added no permanent wealth to the economy. The West African economy became one-dimensional, a fact that severely limited its ability to grow and evolve. Dependent on Europe for slave trade profits and manufactured imports, West Africa lost much of its ability to sustain an economy free of slaving.

With the decline of African political and economic stability came a decline in social and cultural life. The natural flowering of artistic, religious and social traditions withered. In some areas the horrors of the slave trade produced frightening reactions, as in Benin, where priests tried to protect the population from slave raids by making massive human sacrifices. Elsewhere, many Africans committed suicide when faced with the possibility of slavery under the Europeans. The arts declined as master practitioners were kidnapped and shipped to the New World. Ordinary Africans lost some of their freedoms as power and wealth concentrated in the hands of a few warring kings engaged in the slave trade.

Similar political, economic and social conditions arose in East Africa during the 19th century, when Europeans and Americans shifted their focus away from West Africa after abolishing the slave trade there. Everywhere, the effects were the same: African societies lost their economic vitality and political strength. These conditions opened large areas of the continent to European interference. At the same time, the slave trade helped Europeans justify their claims to Africa. They scorned Africans as slaves and slave sellers and came to think of blacks as naturally inferior to whites. The slave trade's most serious impact on Africa lay in the future, with the colonization of the continent by racist nations that owed much of their strength to the traffic in human beings.

THE ABOLITION OF THE SLAVE TRADE

Toward the end of the 18th century, Europeans began to rethink their involvement in the African slave trade. Increasingly vocal protests from antislavery advocates had something to do with shifting opinions on the enterprise, but economics played a more prominent role in the European decision to ban the West African trade officially. The triangular trade, of which slaving was a part, had proved enormously lucrative for the European nations. Profits from the system financed the factories and businesses of the budding Industrial Revolution that would transform the western world's economy in the 19th century.

Simultaneously, the plantations of the New World were becoming less profitable. Their success had created a surplus of sugar in Europe, and while the price of sugar fell the price of slaves went up. Meanwhile, African resistance to the slave trade had sparked attacks on European outposts there, while captives had launched rebellions on board slave ships and in the plantation colonies. The dangers and expense of dealing in slaves became less tolerable as profits went down, so bankers and entrepreneurs turned to new industries, which promised greater income with less risk. The high times of the slave trade had passed.

Starting in the 1790s, the Napoleonic Wars and the French Revolution disrupted trans-Atlantic commerce, further reducing the appeal of slaving. Movements to abolish the slave trade took hold throughout

SIERRA LEONE AND LIBERIA

Two new nations, made up of freed British and American blacks, were founded in Africa during the slave trade era. The first of these, Sierra Leone, was conceived by British abolitionists concerned about the growing numbers of free blacks who were having trouble integrating into English society. In 1787, 411 freed slaves arrived in Africa from England. They were joined a few years later by 1,200 free blacks from Nova Scotia, Canada and about 500 former slaves from Jamaica in the Caribbean. Known as Creoles, the early settlers suffered from tropical diseases and were subject to attacks by indigenous peoples. As English-speaking Christians, they had little in common with African-born blacks.

Great Britain declared Sierra Leone a crown colony in 1808 and used the port of Freetown as the base for its Anti-Slavery Squadron. New arrivals continued to pour into the colony, the majority of them Africans recaptured from slave ships by the squadron. By 1850 about 70,000 "repatriates" settled in Sierra Leone, and the local Creoles managed most governmental and economic affairs. They founded the first African university, Fourah Bay College, in 1827 and sent missionaries into other parts of Africa. As their trade and agriculture flourished, the Creoles intermarried with local peoples and developed a culture that blended Christianity with traditional religions, English with local languages and western ways with African. Increasing British interference in the 1890s reduced Creole

Europe, and in 1804 Denmark outlawed the West African trade. Britain followed suit in 1807, the newly independent United States in 1808, the Netherlands in 1814 and France in 1817. Between 1815 and 1817 Portugal restricted its west coast slavers to areas south of the equator; the export of people from Portuguese-controlled Angola to the Portuguese colony of Brazil continued.

Britain, the most industrially advanced nation at that time, hoped to cultivate Africa as a source of raw materials for industry. Relative peace involvement in the political future of their country, but Sierra Leone continued to cultivate a unique identity.

Just to the south of Sierra Leone, freed blacks from the United States settled Liberia in 1822. They were backed by the American Colonization Society, a white group concerned about the disruptive influence free blacks might have on the American slave population. Although mostly poor, some of the American blacks who founded Liberia had a little education, and most were Christians. They established communities, schools, churches and businesses, declaring their independence from the United States in 1847. Governed by repatriates according to a constitution modeled on that of the United States, Liberia became the second internationally recognized autonomous state in Africa (after Ethiopia). The country gradually incorporated American-born local peoples into its population.

Liberia enjoyed some success in trading during the 19th century, specializing in exporting palm oil, coffee, camwood, sugar, ivory and molasses to Europe. Competition from more powerful European trading companies took its toll on the economy, while internal disputes and corruption troubled the government. Class divisions between the descendants of American-born settlers and local peoples threatened Liberian unity, but the nation held onto its independence even during the period of European partition and colonization. Liberians maintained strong ties with the African-American community and stood as a symbol of freedom for non-African blacks throughout the world.

and stability were required if African nations were to cultivate crops, such as the oil palm, and mine the ores needed by British industry. Britain also hoped to develop the African market for its manufactured goods, an effort that could succeed only in a peaceful region. Aware of the slave trade's destabilizing influence, the British began to police the waters off West Africa and make certain smugglers and other nations stopped exporting slaves. The British "Anti-Slavery Squadron" was dispatched to enforce the international ban on West African slaving and pave the way for "legitimate" European commerce.

Not surprisingly, the demand for African slaves did not end when the West African slave trade was abolished. In the United States, Brazil and Cuba, growing sugar and cotton plantations demanded as many slaves as ever. The number of captives shipped from Africa to these markets actually went up for a few years after the ban went into effect. Some slavers evaded the Anti-Slavery Squadron and continued to operate in West Africa, dealing with kings who still wanted guns and other European goods. The slave smugglers still found a ready supply of slaves from the many African states that had no other source of income. But for the most part, the African slave trade shifted to the east coast, where it remained legal.

American slavers became the major players in the 19th-century slave trade. Along with the remaining British traders, they sailed to the Swahili city-states ruled by the Omani Arabs. Mozambique and Zanzibar were the two main slaving ports of the 1800s. Arab and Swahili traders brought slaves to these ports from the interior, usually forcing them to carry ivory destined for export as well. During the 1830s and 1840s, the peak years of the East African slave trade, as many as 60,000 people a year were taken from the region. About half of them went to Arabia and the Middle East and half went to the Americas. As in West Africa, the warfare and depopulation that accompanied slaving wreaked havoc on certain East African societies.

Despite the official European abolition of the East African slave trade in 1873, slavers continued to ship Africans overseas until slavery itself was abolished throughout Europe and the Americas. The trade finally petered out around 1888; before it did, a total of nearly 2 million slaves were exported in the 19th century alone. When the slaving stopped, many African societies were left in shambles. Others survived the onslaught in better condition, particularly interior cultures out of the direct path of the slave trade. The slave trade had brought sub-Saharan Africa into contact with the modern world, but almost without exception Africans did not benefit from the change. Instead, the European nations gained a firm foothold from which to surge into the continent and divide it among themselves.

THE ROOTS OF APARTHEID IN SOUTHERN AFRICA, PRE-1870

Thinly populated southern Africa largely escaped the predations of European slavers. Indeed, except for the treacherous seas along its coast, the area attracted little European notice before the middle of the 17th century. The widely scattered Khoikhoi and San populations produced none of the gold, ivory, spices or other goods sought by oceangoing merchants. For 150 years, Europeans viewed southern Africa as nothing more than an inconvenient obstacle to be passed on their way to and from the Indian Ocean. They did not develop the extensive trading ties with the local people that formed the basis of the West African slave trade. But southern Africa would endure its own suffering at European hands.

Portuguese, Dutch, French and British ships sailing between Europe and Asia found the Cape of Good Hope (originally called the Cape of Storms) a convenient stopover on their long journey. Located at the midpoint of the trading route, the cape offered fresh water, timber and foodstuffs to replenish the ships' supplies. Early on, European sailors started trading with Khoikhoi pastoralists for cattle at Table Bay. The commerce was sporadic, as the Khoikhoi were willing to part only with their surplus, aged or sick livestock. On occasion, when the Khoikhoi refused to supply as many head of cattle as the ships demanded, sailors raided Khoikhoi herds and took what they wanted. As the number of ships stopping at the cape grew, cattle became increasingly difficult to come by and tensions between Europeans and Khoikhoi increased. It was at this point that Europeans decided to establish a permanent presence in southern Africa.

THE FIRST BOERS

Hoping to stabilize the supply of meat to its own ships as well as to protect its access to the valuable sea routes and to profit from the provisioning of other ships, the Dutch East India Company established a small outpost on the cape in 1652. Operated by soldiers, the settlement also grew a variety of crops for sale to the seafarers. The company intended to keep the enterprise small and separate from the surrounding Khoikhoi and San communities, but as shipping traffic increased the demand for supplies grew. In 1657, when company gardens and cattle trading could no longer meet the demand, the company released some of the soldiers from service to set up large farms worked by slaves.

The company encouraged Dutch settlers to move to southern Africa to grow crops in the territory around Cape Town. Called Boers (*boer* is the Dutch word for "farmer"), these settlers brought with them a firm religious belief that they were chosen by God to take southern Africa from the "barbarians" and establish a Christian colony. Their descendants in modern South Africa call themselves Afrikaners and speak a Dutch-derived language called Afrikans. The Boers derisively named the Khoikhoi "Hottentots" and the San "Bushmen" and claimed large tracts of those peoples' land for their farms. At the same time, the company pressured the Khoikhoi to provide more and more cattle, in exchange for which they offered Dutch goods, such as beads or liquor, of little real value; the Dutch refused to trade firearms to the Khoikhoi.

Those Khoikhoi who refused to trade with the Dutch were subjected to cattle raids. Before long, the area around Cape Town was drained of cattle and the company pushed farther into Khoikhoi territory. Khoikhoi uprisings in 1659 and 1660 failed, and both the Boers and the

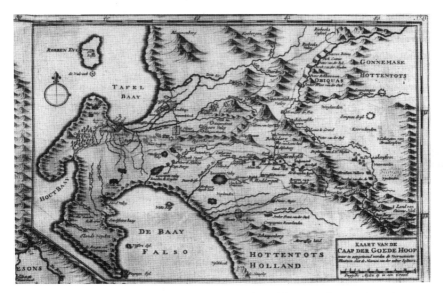

Map showing Dutch settlement at the Cape of Good Hope about 1700. (Picture Collection, The Branch Libraries, The New York Public Library)

company claimed the "right of conquest" to Khoikhoi and San land. Despite centuries-old occupation of the region by Khoisan-speaking peoples, the Dutch settlers considered the land empty and free for the taking, much as European settlers in North America viewed Native American territory. The Khoikhoi and the San were pushed east and north as the European presence on the cape expanded, but not without a fight. Between 1673 and 1677, the Khoi/Dutch War unfolded in a series of skirmishes and cattle raids. Equipped with guns and horses, the Dutch emerged victorious.

After the Khoi/Dutch War, Boer settlement swelled rapidly, with the company's encouragement. Any Boer who was interested in farming could rent large tracts of land from the company at nominal expense. In the temperate climate, similar to that of the Mediterranean region, wheat, grapes and other produce thrived. A serious labor shortage plagued the company farms, however, because few whites would work for others when they could so easily acquire farms of their own. The Khoikhoi and San made unwilling laborers, so the company imported slaves from Mozambique, Madagascar and Indonesia. Boer farmers started large families and new settlers continued to arrive; the number of Boer farms climbed. By 1700 Boer farmers produced three times as much food as the company required for its Cape Town supply station. The Boers suddenly found their opportunities under the company limited.

In search of new ways to make a living, Boers started emigrating from the company's domain into Khoikhoi and San territory. They packed their belongings into ox-drawn wagons and ventured eastward up the coast, earning the label *trekboers* (*trek* is the Dutch word for "pull"). Hunting for elephants and other game, trading with the Khoikhoi for cattle, and setting up cattle ranches of their own, the trekboers forced the Khoikhoi into less desirable territory. Some Khoikhoi, stripped of their cattle, went to work for the Boers as servants and laborers. The San, who raided Boer herds and otherwise offended the white settlers, were considered vermin to be exterminated. The Boers hunted them almost to extinction. Reluctant to get involved in conflicts with African peoples, and planning to keep whites and blacks geographically and politically separate, the company discouraged the trekboer expansion. The Boers, however, shrugged off the company's restrictions and kept moving.

A 19th-century depiction of a trekboer wagon and its long train of oxen. (Mansell Collection, London)

The trekboer expansion eastward took white settlers toward land watered by monsoon rains that came off the Indian Ocean. Because much of the coast between Cape Town and the Drakensberg Mountain region was quite arid, the Boers were forced to disperse widely with their herds. Boer families believed they required about 6,000 acres (2,500 hectares) of land apiece on which to graze their cattle. When Boer sons reached adulthood and married, they each expected to take over a similar estate. Because the early Boers had large families and often moved to new ranches when they exhausted their pastures, soon they occupied a very large area of southeastern Africa.

Everywhere they went, the trekboers met resistance from Khoikhoi guerrillas. To fight the Africans, the Boers formed mounted commando units that launched swift, brutal attacks. The combination of guns, horses and African susceptibility to European diseases almost always spelled defeat for the Khoikhoi. Those who survived began to retreat to the north along with the San, out of the path of Boer expansion. If they stayed too long in Boer-dominated areas, their cattle was taken, often along with their children.

It was a Boer practice to kidnap Khoikhoi children and put them to work as unpaid "apprentices," basically slaves, until they were well into adulthood. Even Khoikhoi who went to work for the Boers as adults were treated as little more than slaves. With few options other than to work for the white invaders, a non-European underclass composed of Khoikhoi, freed slaves and people of mixed race developed in the Boer settlements. Its members were relegated to subservient status and allowed few rights.

Late in the 1760s the leading edge of trekboer expansion reached the western border of Xhosa territory, located on the coastland, or Zuurveld, east of the Drakensberg Mountains. The Xhosa themselves had been expanding westward and arrived on the southwestern Zuurveld at the same time the Boers did. At first, both groups moved cautiously into the area, the Boers establishing large ranches and the Xhosa grazing the land between the ranches. But as the Boers claimed more and more land, they squeezed the Xhosa onto smaller and smaller pastures. Throughout the 1770s the Boers and Xhosa met in numerous skirmishes. The Boers continued to press up the coast, but the company, fearing more violence, forbad them from crossing the official Dutch border.

The insatiable Boer hunger for African land, however, finally sparked full-scale war in 1779. This war, between the Boers and the Xhosa, was the first of the Frontier Wars, also known as the Kaffir Wars. (The Boers called black Africans *kaffirs*, a word derived from the Arabic term *kafir*, meaning "infidel." They picked up the term from the Portuguese of the east coast.) Intense and bloody, the war ended in stalemate in 1781. There would be eight more Frontier Wars over the next century. The second occurred in 1793 as a Boer reaction to the continuing westward push of the Xhosa. Because it threatened the company's already declining prosperity, the Boers' inclination to battle Africans for land met with company disapproval. The company intervened in the second war and signed a treaty with the Xhosa, which angered the Boers.

Boer discontent with company policies led to rebellion in 1795. Trekboers living hundreds of miles from Cape Town declared their independence from the company and established a republic. In response, the company stopped trading with the Boers. Without essential supplies, available only from the company, the Boers could not sustain their rebellion. The first Boer republic collapsed, as the company's authority over southern Africa would soon do.

THE BRITISH IN CAPE COLONY

In 1795 control of the cape passed from Dutch to British hands. The company's hold on the region had been weakening for some time, and the British saw the cape as a valuable strategic acquisition. Because Britain was at war with France between 1793 and 1815, the British hoped they could block French access to Indian Ocean trading routes with a military base in Cape Town. But the British had the same problems governing the Boers as the Dutch had had. In 1799, when the Boers launched a second uprising, the British had to divert valuable military resources to suppressing it. They also had to defend the eastern border against African incursions. The third Frontier War (1800–03), in which the Khoikhoi joined with the Xhosa against the Europeans, proved an especially hard-won victory. Finding the cape more trouble than it seemed worth, the British returned it to the Dutch in 1803.

Nevertheless, Britain took the cape from the Dutch a second time in 1806. The British needed a port of call for the growing numbers of ships they sent to and from India, and they needed a base from which they could defend their interests in the sea routes. To secure their position on the cape, the British instituted a number of reforms meant to stabilize the colony. The Boers of Cape Colony, as it was now called, resented British meddling in their customary ways of operating. For instance, when the West African slave trade was abolished in 1807, the British colonial government instituted the 1809 Hottentot Code to regulate relations between white settlers and black laborers. Employers were required to give their workers contracts, and employees were permitted to sue their bosses for mistreatment. The code was far from humanitarian, though: Nonwhites were also required to carry passes identifying their employment status, and whites could force anyone without a pass to work for them. But the Boers resented the few protections the British did extend to Africans.

Although the Boers complained of British reforms, they benefited from the British military presence on the frontier. In 1811 and 1812, in the fourth Frontier War, British troops evicted the Xhosa from new territory desired by trekboers on the eastern coast. They pushed the Xhosa even farther east in the fifth Frontier War (1818–19) despite fierce resistance from the outgunned Africans. These moves profited the trekboers in the area, but Britain found the expense increasingly intolerable.

After the conclusion of the Napoleonic Wars in 1815, the British closed some of their military garrisons in Cape Colony and imported about 5,000 English settlers to solidify the British position in southern Africa. The colonial government continued to pass laws protecting the rights of non-Europeans in an effort to prevent further development of the racial caste system that the Boers had been fostering. Christian missionaries working on behalf of Africans persuaded the authorities to lift various restrictions on blacks in 1828, winning them the right to choose their employers and work their own farms. Finally, in 1833, Cape Colony freed all slaves under its jurisdiction.

Further angering the Boers, the British left much of the responsibility for border defense in Boer hands. Rather than maintaining troops at the border of white territory, the British tried to establish a buffer zone of uninhabited land between the Boers and the Xhosa. Neither frontier group paid attention to British prohibitions on settling in the zone, however, and conflicts developed between the squatters. A rising tide of violence turned into the sixth Frontier War in 1834, forcing the British to intervene. After British troops annexed the remaining Xhosa lands, the war came to an end in 1835. The following year, much to Boer dismay, the British decided to return some of the land taken from the Xhosa. The move turned the stream of Boers trekking away from British territory into a flood.

THE BOER TREK TO INDEPENDENCE

Many Boers deeply resented what they viewed as British softness toward the indigenous population of southern Africa. Exacerbated by linguistic, religious and other cultural disparities between the two European groups, the differences in their racial attitudes seemed irreconcilable. While the British were hardly racial revolutionaries, they believed in basic, if restricted, human rights for Africans, whom they felt needed European "protection." The Boers, meanwhile, believed in the natural superiority of whites over blacks and of "Christians" over Africans, and in their right to subjugate their "inferiors." They wished to pursue their own policies concerning the "proper" treatment of people of color, which included compulsory, unpaid labor. Any British moves on behalf of Africans seemed to the Boers like a direct assault on their divinely sanctioned way of life.

About 1836 or 1837, Boers started packing their possessions into ox-drawn wagons and moving out of areas controlled by the British. They sought to free themselves of interference from outsiders and to gain access to more land. Known as voortrekkers (literally, front-trekkers), the migrant Boers traveled in relatively small groups. Although about 14,000 Boers joined the push into the interior in its first decade, the movement was not the organized "Great Trek" later glorified by the Afrikaners. Guided by their personal objectives, individual Boer families spread into regions depopulated by the Mfecane/Difaqane, the interkingdom wars that ravaged southeastern Africa in the early 19th century. Natal, the coastal area south of Zulu territory, and the eastern high veld just across the Drakensberg Mountains were the two most popular destinations.

Though the Boers avoided areas of dense African settlement, they often had to fight the people whose lands they invaded. At first, they lost many battles against the highly trained African armies of the region. The mighty Zulu all but wiped out the voortrekkers in 1838, but the migrants learned from their defeats and devised highly effective defense techniques. Among these was the *laager*, a fortified camp in which wagons were drawn into an easily defended circle. The Boers also used mounted commandos to raid and scatter small encampments of Africans. On occasion, they formed alliances with some Africans to fight a mutual enemy. By these means, the Boers managed to defeat forces far larger than their own. They avoided the heart of Zulu territory and never completely eliminated Africans from areas they claimed, but they succeeded in establishing a permanent presence.

The Boers of Natal promptly declared themselves an independent republic, but British authorities continued to consider all Boers British subjects. Worried about the impact of Boer activity on their interests, especially at Port of Natal (now Durban), the British refused to recognize the republic's independence. Boer occupation of the port posed a threat to British control of Indian Ocean trading routes. To eliminate that threat, the British annexed the Boer republic of Natal in 1843 and proclaimed it a British colony. Boers moved out of the area, crossing the Drakensberg Mountains and dispersing across the high veld.

On the high veld, the Boers again declared their independence and founded two republics: the South African Republic (Transvaal) and the Orange Free State. Unwilling to pursue its expensive struggle to control the Boers, Britain recognized the independence of the republics in 1852 and 1854, respectively. In 1853, meanwhile, Britain granted Cape Colony a constitution and allowed it to elect a Parliament that reported to the British Parliament in London. About 3,000 German settlers who agreed to serve in the British Foreign Legion arrived during the 1850s; a smaller number of Irish immigrants also landed in Cape Colony. By then, the white population of southern Africa numbered about 300,000, compared with 1 or 2 million blacks.

Cape Colony turned much of its agriculture to sheep farming and prospered on the income from wool exporting. The colony of Natal, populated by British immigrants, thrived as a source of sugar. The Boer republics, by contrast, remained relatively poor. Located on dry, easily exhausted grassland, the South African Republic and the Orange Free State needed to expand constantly in order to maintain a minimum of adequate pasturage. Boer expansion on the high veld continued, fanning the flames of warfare almost constantly. Neither the Boers nor the indigenous Sotho could afford the nonstop fighting, which severely sapped their resources. In 1843 Moshoeshoe, king of Basotho, applied to the British for protection, which they granted. In 1871 Moshoeshoe's kingdom was annexed by Cape Colony.

The British intervention in Basotho relieved the Boers of much of the pressure arising from their invasion of African lands. Starting about 1870 the Boers turned their attention from expansion to internal development and began to build a stronger economy. Those African kingdoms that had survived the arrival of whites tried to carry on their traditional ways. Robbed of their herds and land, other Africans either went to work as farmers and hunters for the Boers or moved to dismal "reserves" set aside for them in British territory. The fragile coexistence of British colonies, Boer republics and displaced Africans lasted only a few years, however. Discovery of diamonds north of the Orange River and then of gold in the Transvaal would soon set off a new colonial frenzy that would once again change the map of southern Africa.

CONQUERING THE "DARK CONTINENT"

With the official end of the West African slave trade in the first two decades of the 19th century, Africans and Europeans alike began seeking new commodities that could be traded along the well-established networks. Europe hoped to develop Africa as a market for the manufactured goods pouring out of its new factories; Africa hoped to import modern goods and technology to rebuild its economy. But the relationship between the two continents was no longer one of equal trading partners. The huge profits Europe made in the slave trade had propelled it into the industrial age, while the end of the slave trade deprived many African civilizations of their only source of income. Europe, now far more advanced than Africa technologically, economically and militarily, began to gain the upper hand on the global scene.

By 1800, the slave trade and its impact in Africa had convinced many Europeans of their innate superiority to Africans. The official end of the trade left many African cultures in political and economic chaos. Some Europeans assumed the war, famine and instability that plagued many societies of early 19th-century coastal Africa were the natural and perpetual conditions of African life. The havoc wreaked by European exploitation was now used as an excuse for continued intervention; the myths about "savage Africa" that had been used to justify the slave trade were now used to justify increasing European control over African life. Just as slavers had rationalized their activities as a means of "rescuing" Africans from "barbarism," now Europeans claimed they knew what was best for the inhabitants of the "Dark Continent" and had an obligation to interfere in African affairs.

Of course, the real motivation for European activity in Africa was still money. Operating in tandem with the profit motive was the largely Protestant desire to bring the message of Christianity to the Africans. And in order to open new arenas for merchants and missionaries, Europeans decided to explore the continent and chart its geography. From the 1790s onward, European explorers began to penetrate the African interior, missionaries set up stations along the coasts and merchants pursued new avenues of commerce. Advances and contacts made by each group fostered the interests of the other, and together all three promoted the infiltration of European culture into Africa. In the first three quarters of the 19th century, merchants, missionaries and explorers laid the groundwork for the European empire in Africa.

DEVELOPING "LEGITIMATE COMMERCE"

Although smugglers continued to export large numbers of African captives until the 1880s, after the West African slave trade was outlawed most European traders set their sights on what they termed "legitimate commerce." They had to seek new trading opportunities in Africa because by 1800 the continent had become an important market for European goods—a market the merchants could not afford to lose. Some of the smaller powers, such as the Danes and the Dutch, had to drop out of the market because they did not have the resources to develop new opportunities. The larger nations, most notably the British and the French, entered the new era enthusiastically. Britain had badly hurt French interests around the Senegal River during the Napoleonic Wars of 1793 to 1815, and France was determined to keep its rival from achieving a monopoly over trade with West Africa.

Because the extensive trading networks of the slaving era remained in place, West Africa attracted a good deal of European attention as a post–slave trade partner. But many of the large kingdoms that had built their fortunes on slaving were unable to adapt to the new conditions. The British and French found their most viable contacts among the small city-states and independent operators who quickly learned to supply the gum arabic, palm oil, palm kernels, coffee, cocoa and peanuts the Europeans wanted. Although gold remained a sought-after prize, palm oil, desired in Europe as a lubricant for machinery, became the most lucrative export. Competition among suppliers was fierce, a situation exacerbated by attempts on the part of larger kingdoms to take over the interests of smaller ones. The governments of Britain and France soon intervened.

French activity centered around the gum arabic and peanut trade along the Senegal River and extended south and east to the areas now occupied by Guinea, the Ivory Coast and Gabon. The British, meanwhile, focused their attention on the Gold Coast and the Niger River delta, known as the "Oil Rivers" because it served as the main transport route for palm oil on its way to the coast. Both nations had already established a naval presence along the coast of West Africa to enforce the antislaving laws, Britain using Sierra Leone as the base for its patrolling activities. Early on, each nation negotiated treaties with local rulers for land on which to build forts and trading posts and for protected access to trade with the interior. British and French consuls arrived to mediate relations between Europeans and Africans as well as to resolve disputes among African competitors.

Much as they had done for centuries, for the first half of the 1800s European traders stayed on the coast and traded for goods brought from the interior by traveling merchants. They dreamed of boosting profits by cutting out these traders and making direct contact with suppliers in the interior, but they knew nothing of the trading routes. Then, in 1830, Englishmen John and Richard Lander discovered the mouth of the Niger River, a highway to the interior. The recent invention of commercial steamships made large-scale navigation of the river by Europeans possible; in 1832–34 and again in 1841–42 the British sent steamship expeditions up the Niger to explore. Both missions were defeated by malaria, the mosquito-borne disease that felled most Europeans who ventured into the interior. Until the 1850 discovery of quinine as an antimalaria remedy, Europeans in Africa were confined to the coast.

In 1857 the British started launching regular merchant steamers up the Niger River and established consulates in the interior. By then they had bought the Danish forts on the Gold Coast (they would acquire the Dutch forts in 1872) and formed an alliance with the Fante against the Asante, whose continuing involvement in the slave trade threatened British interests. In this way the British established informal authority over the area, where frequent conflict among local rulers had eroded traditional political structures. War also prevailed among the palm-oil growers of the Niger delta, allowing the British to extend their influence there.

African leaders seeking to consolidate their control over trade in the area relied on the British for guns and ammunition. If they wanted to maintain good relations with arms suppliers, these leaders had to make numerous concessions to British concerns. Through ambitious African rulers Britain came to exert its will over the Gold Coast and the Niger delta. But the British felt they could not rely on their African partners to control the situation in West Africa. They wanted to break the power of the African merchants and take complete control of trading activity. In spite of great resistance from the Africans, the British decided to establish a permanent outpost. In 1851 they captured the city of Lagos and made it their autonomous base in the area. In 1861 they annexed it to the British empire as a Crown colony.

The French pursued an even more aggressive policy along the Senegal River. After a brief, unsuccessful attempt to establish plantations in the area, they set up a series of posts from which to trade with local people and protect the area from British expansion. In 1854 Louis Faidherbe was appointed consul and given orders to develop trade to its fullest potential. Under his leadership, the French occupied Cape Verde (now Dakar) in 1857. Faidherbe recruited an army of Africans commanded by French officers to establish military control over the region that supplied French merchants. Backed by this army, French traders ventured up the Senegal in the 1860s, extending European influence. Faidherbe's system allowed the French both to give special training to the Africans working for them and to establish a permanent presence in the region.

The pursuit of "legitimate commerce" followed a similar pattern in East Africa. The British and French were interested in the area largely due to its importance to ships sailing to and from India and the East Indies. Neither nation wanted the other to gain dominance in the Indian Ocean, so both maintained ties to East Africa. The French set up a coaling station for its ships at Obok (in present-day Djibouti), which would later serve as their foothold for establishing a colony in Somali territory. In Ethiopia, a lively trade in ivory and firearms developed, and the British established a consulate. The British gained some influence in Ethiopian affairs in 1868, when they retaliated against Emperor Tewodros II for his mistreatment of two British officers. Tewodros committed suicide when the British defeated him in battle, and two successors subsequently jostled for power under Britain's watchful eye.

British influence in East Africa grew steadily in the 19th century, soon surpassing that of the French. In an effort to gain an edge over the French in the Indian Ocean, to put an end to the slave trade there and to tap the abundant ivory resources of the region, the British established diplomatic relations with the sultan of Zanzibar, who controlled east-coast trade. Britain established a consulate at Zanzibar in 1840 and negotiated a series of agreements with the sultan to halt slaving along Africa's east coast. But the sultan seemed unable to stop the slavers, and the British assumed a larger role in the task. By the 1860s the sultan was little more than a puppet of the British government, with little choice but to do their bidding. The British got directly involved in interior trading during the 1870s, when they launched merchant steamships on the extensive network of lakes and rivers there.

Throughout the 19th century, the British and French competed for dominance in North Africa as well. Long controlled by Muslims, and largely part of the Ottoman Empire based in Turkey, North Africa had been virtually closed to the Christian nations of Europe for centuries. Western scientists or merchants interested in traveling to the region had had to disguise themselves in Arab garb in order to gain access. But with the introduction of steamships, the Europeans built strong navies on the Mediterranean Sea, capable of overpowering the sailing navy of the Ottoman Empire. North African countries seeking greater independence from their Ottoman occupiers cultivated friendly relations with the Europeans, especially the two great powers, France and

Britain. Only the autonomous kingdom of Morocco, suspicious of European intentions, cut off its relations with the outside world.

Egypt became the main theater for British and French involvement in North Africa. A series of Egyptian rulers intent on modernizing the country invited European advisers, military officers and bureaucrats into the country, installing many in government posts. When restrictions against foreign business interests were dropped in 1838, European merchants poured into the country. Borrowing extensively from European allies, the Egyptians improved irrigation, education, public facilities and the army. During the 1850s the British built an extensive network of railroads linking Alexandria, Cairo and the Gulf of Suez. These routes shortened the trip between England and its colony in India by eliminating the need to sail around Africa's southern tip: Passengers and goods could now take steamships across the Mediterranean, travel by rail to the Gulf of Suez and sail down the Red Sea to the Indian Ocean.

Not content to let the British lead the way in Egypt, the French in 1854 acquired the right to build a canal across the Isthmus of Suez, linking the Mediterranean with the Red Sea. Financial difficulties and opposition from the British delayed the start of the project for five years, but in 1859 work got underway. When it opened in 1869, the canal became an instant success, proving especially beneficial to the British steamship lines. The canal did little to enhance Egypt's political or economic power, for aside from a block of shares owned by the government it was entirely controlled by foreigners. And Egypt soon lost its shares in the canal, when the bankrupt government sold them to the British. In the 1870s, Egypt's efforts to expand up the Nile into the Sudan left it badly overextended and vulnerable to further European interference. In Egypt, as in the rest of Africa, the European pursuit of "legitimate commerce" laid the foundations of colonialism.

IMPORTING EUROPEAN CULTURE

While 19th-century Europeans exported their goods and political influence to Africa via "legitimate commerce," they exported their beliefs via Christian missionaries. Catholic missionaries had gone to the continent soon after the first Portuguese adventurers, but the Africans quickly expelled or killed most of them. African rulers, recognizing that

THE FRENCH IN ALGERIA

Long before the 19th century, France and Algeria enjoyed a solid trading relationship in which Algeria exported grain and olive oil in exchange for manufactured goods. That relationship began to sour after Napoleon's occupation of Egypt between 1798 and 1801, for which Algeria provisioned the French army. Troubled by a series of wars and internal problems, France was slow to pay Algeria for the goods; the Algerians eventually lost their patience. Algeria and France broke off diplomatic relations in 1827.

At that time, French king Louis XVIII and his successor, Charles X, were looking for a triumph on the international front to divert their angry subjects' attention from domestic problems. In 1830, declaring that France would end Algerian corsairing (piracy) on the Mediterranean, Charles X captured the port of Algiers. The city had served as a base for corsairs in the past, but in fact the practice of piracy had nearly ended before the French intervened. Nonetheless, the victory enhanced French prestige. It did little for Charles X, however, who was deposed soon after the invasion.

By 1834 the French had set up a colonial administration throughout the strip of coastline between the mountains and the sea. Distressed by the incursion of Christian colonizers, the nomadic Muslims of the interior launched a jihad against the French. France pushed into the Algerian interior to put down the uprising, encountering fierce resistance and employing brutal tactics against the Algerians. In 1848 France declared Algeria a part of France, but the fighting continued. French soldiers destroyed countless homes and farms and killed perhaps hundreds of thousands of people before extending their control to the northern edge of the Sahara in 1879. By then, several hundred thousand French colonists and soldiers lived in Algeria. They would not leave until nearly a century later.

Christianity would undermine the traditional religious basis of their authority, fought its spread. Only among the Kongo did Catholic missionaries make any headway, and that was just temporarily; Catholicism was quickly absorbed into the local belief system.

An evangelical revival among late-18th- and early-19th-century European and North American Protestants spurred efforts to try missionary work in Africa again. Viewing Christianity as a weapon against the slave trade that still thrived in Africa, Protestants formed missionary societies to bring "salvation" to people they believed had no religion. Among the most prominent were three British groups: the London Missionary Society, which arrived in southern Africa in 1799; and the Church Missionary Society and the Wesleyan Methodist Missionary Society, which launched their efforts from Sierra Leone starting in 1804 and 1811, respectively. These societies, and many others from England, France, Germany, the Netherlands and the United States, devoted themselves not only to ending the slave trade and preaching the word of God, but to encouraging Africans to adopt European clothing and customs.

Throughout the first half of the 19th century, European missionaries had little success in Africa. Generally sent to areas where Europeans of the same nationality already lived, they found some converts among "Europeanized" Africans, such as those on the Gold Coast. Among displaced peoples, such as the freed slaves of Sierra Leone or the uprooted Khoikhoi and San of southern Africa, Christian missionaries also managed to make some gains. But most of these Africans were not primarily interested in the missionaries' religious message. Instead, they saw the missionaries as potential trading partners, educators and allies against hostile African or European outsiders. Some rulers who saw the benefits of modernization embraced the European ways promoted by the missionaries and allowed them to set up schools where Africans learned how to read. Although missionaries fostered literacy for the sole purpose of giving Africans access to the Bible, the impact of education was much wider.

Christian missionaries made some inroads in West Africa, where they worked among settlements of freed slaves (such as those in Sierra Leone, Liberia, the British-run community on Fernando Po Island and the French-administered Libreville in Gabon). These people had had previous exposure to Christianity. These areas served as launching pads for the expansion of missionary work throughout West Africa, particularly in present-day Nigeria and Cameroon. The missionaries often trained African converts to spread the gospel, and these educated African Christians made a significant impact in pockets of West Africa. Southern Africa also saw some missionary success, although not in the Boer republics, which repudiated missionaries' efforts to help Africans. In southern Africa, as in West Africa, the missionaries offered education and technical training to converts. An educated, "Europeanized" black elite began to prosper in western and southern Africa.

Many Africans, however, were hostile to European missionaries. With their new, white God and their strictures against dancing, nonreligious singing, polygamy, nudity and ritual, the missionaries condemned most of the traditions that bound African society together and gave chiefs their power. Some kingdoms, such as Asante, Dahomey and Benin, resisted the missionaries' efforts in every way. Until the final quarter of the 19th century, in fact, Christian missionaries effected

African children in a school run by white missionaries, 19th century. (Picture Collection, The Branch Libraries, The New York Public Library)

little real religious change in Africa, and virtually none outside the coastal areas.

Despite the efforts of missionaries, slavery persisted within Africa and the slave trade continued. Africans continued to practice their traditions and religions. Frustrated missionaries began to call for assistance from European governments in the campaign to "civilize" Africa. As the growing imbalance in economic power put more political influence in the hands of Europeans, and as Europeans came to view Africans as in need of help and protection, the missionaries' calls for direct intervention in African affairs gained an audience. Europeans began to consider colonization a justifiable, even obligatory next step in their relationship with Africa.

DRAWING A MAP FOR EMPIRE

In order to extend their trading and missionary enterprises—and hence, their influence—beyond the familiar coastal areas, Europeans needed to learn what lay in the interior of the "Dark Continent." Starting with the major rivers of West Africa, European explorers began to investigate the geography of Africa in the late 18th century. The Scottish adventurer James Bruce visited Ethiopia as early as 1768, but when he returned to Europe in 1783 telling of that kingdom's riches and grandeur, he was dismissed as a crank. In 1788 a group of wealthy Englishmen founded the Association for the Discovery of the Interior Parts of Africa, known as the Africa Association. Its immediate goal was to explore the Niger River and find the city of Timbuktu, long rumored to be immensely wealthy. Its backers hoped to open up lucrative new trading opportunities on the basis of the "discoveries" made by its agents.

The Africa Association sent three expeditions to West Africa before succeeding with a British explorer by the name of Mungo Park, who charted parts of the Niger River in 1795–97 and again in 1805–06. Park's triumph launched the age of European exploration; adventurers of all nationalities and all motivations poured into Africa in search of glory. Accompanied by large caravans of African employees, most European explorers traveled established trade routes and relied on African guides to show the way. Still, when they became the first whites to reach a given destination and returned to tell about it, they gained the status of heroes.

In 1827 a Frenchman became the first European to reach Timbuktu and return; in 1830 two Englishmen found the mouth of the Niger River, opening it to European navigation. In 1847–49, two German explorers became the first white men to see the snowcapped peaks of Mt. Kilimanjaro and Mt. Kenya in East Africa. Perhaps the most famous of all European explorers, the English missionary David Livingstone traveled north from Cape Colony in the 1840s, reaching Lozi territory along the upper Zambezi River in 1851. Between 1852 and 1856 Livingstone marched west to Luanda on the coast of modern Angola and then east down the Zambezi River valley to the coast of Mozambique, becoming the first European to traverse the continent.

When malaria, the great barrier to European expansion into the African interior, was conquered by quinine in 1850, the pace of exploration accelerated. That year, the African Association renamed itself the Royal Geographical Society. Henry Barth, a German, finished charting the course of the Niger River and pressed through the Sudan into the Sahara. Others, meanwhile, turned their attention to Africa's other great rivers: the Nile, the Zambezi and the Congo (now Zaire). Between 1858 and 1864 David Livingstone steamed up the Zambezi River, came upon and named Victoria Falls (which blocked further passage up the river) and turned up the Shire River to Lake Malawi. Livingstone's findings piqued European curiosity about East and Central Africa; more explorers pressed into the region.

The Royal Geographical Society sent Richard Burton and John Speke up the Nile to Lake Tanganyika from 1856 to 1859, then sent Speke and James Grant to Lake Victoria Nyasa, the source of the Nile, in 1862–64. When Livingstone set off on an expedition in 1866 and was not heard from for years, an American newspaper publisher seeking publicity sent the British explorer H. M. Stanley to find him. Stanley met Livingstone at Lake Tanganyika in 1871, two years before Livingstone's death deep in the African interior. In 1874 Stanley set out on another expedition, leaving from Zanzibar. He traveled to Buganda and then down the Congo River to its mouth on the Atlantic Coast. Along the way he and his porters killed many Africans who resisted the invasion of their homelands by whites.

By 1875 European explorers mapped out a fairly complete picture of the African interior. From this point forward, explorers became the

Stanley's descent of the Congo River. (Peter Newark's Historical Pictures)

direct agents of colonial expansion, as European nations began to jockey for possession of African lands. One such explorer was Stanley, whom King Leopold II of Belgium recruited in 1878 to lead another expedition along the Congo. Stanley's duties included establishing trading and diplomatic posts and signing treaties with local peoples to prepare the region for annexation by the king. Within a few years the area opened by Stanley became the Congo Free State under King Leopold II's rule.

Mercantile, missionary and geographical activity in Africa benefited few Africans and harmed many more; yet they had clear short-term advantages for Europeans. Gradually, success in all three areas sparked European interest in direct control over the continent. Before the 1870s, Europeans had had little interest in extensive involvement in African politics. But once the first Europeans made the move toward colonialism, the other nations rushed to claim a piece of a continent that did not, in fact, belong to them. "The scramble" was on.

PARTITION AND COLONIZATION, 1870–1900

Throughout the 19th century, as many European nations underwent rapid industrialization, they increasingly looked to Africa as a market for their manufactured goods and as a potentially rich source of raw materials. Growing competition among Europeans for access to Africa eventually prompted them to transform their established trading partnerships with Africans into relationships of subjugation. Most often through trickery or force, Europeans gained control of much of Africa's economy; from there, it was only a short step to political dominance. Two historical facts contributed significantly to Europe's rising strength in Africa: First, in the 19th century, many African kingdoms experienced serious internal disruptions and frequent wars against rivals. Europeans took advantage of the instability, playing African rivals against each other until both sides were so weakened that whites could step in and take over. Second, European military technology advanced rapidly in the 19th century, and most Europeans were careful not to allow their most sophisticated weaponry to fall into African hands. The two weapons that spelled doom for Africa were artillery, used for bombardment, and the Maxim gun, the first mobile machine gun.

Once a few European nations established the first colonies on African soil, others swept down to claim a share of the continent. Possession of African colonies became a point of national prestige among European nations. The last three decades of the 1800s, when white nations rushed to beat out their rivals for African holdings, came to be known as the era of "the scramble." At first, many European governments assigned the task of governing their "protectorates" to concessionary companies, such as the Royal Niger Company and the Imperial British East Africa Company. In exchange for expanding and developing the territories, these companies were permitted to draw a profit from mining, trade and other activities. The concessionary companies violently exploited Africans and focused on short-term profit instead of long-term growth. When the necessity of tighter control became apparent, white governments took over the job of direct administration.

The colonizers justified their greed and brutality by asserting that they "knew what was best" for the Africans, whose supposed lesser intelligence and moral inferiority required that they be treated as children. During the 1880s and 1890s, Europeans signed numerous treaties among themselves defining the borders of their new possessions. Africans, of course, saw the move to colonization as nothing more than blatant aggression. Realizing that white colonial expansion would rob them of political autonomy and control of interior trade, they launched dozens of diplomatic and military efforts to stave off the European incursion. They discovered that Europeans rarely honored treaties of friendship and cooperation signed with African leaders. The only choices were to submit or to fight; and most Africans did not choose to give up their independence without a battle. Armed African resistance to European conquest was especially fierce during the 1890s.

EUROPEAN CONTROL OF NORTH AFRICA

European dominance in North Africa began with the French invasion of Algiers in 1830. By 1879 the French had secured most of the area now occupied by modern Algeria and had started the push to take over the rest of the region. They had no luck with Morocco, a sensitive prize because of its location across from Spain on the Gibraltar Strait, the narrow passageway between the Mediterranean Sea and the Atlantic

Ocean. No European dared invade Morocco in the 1800s, for doing so promised to provoke protest, and perhaps retaliation, from the other powers. Even if this were not the case, Morocco's long tradition of independent nationhood and its stout xenophobia (fear of foreigners) made invasion risky. The westernmost country of al-Maghrib would retain its independence until 1912.

France looked eastward instead, to the ailing Ottoman province of Tunisia. In a story similar to that of Egypt, Tunisia's ambitious program of modernization and expansion had plunged it deep into debt to various European nations. The provincial government, only loosely connected to Ottoman rulers in Turkey, went bankrupt in 1869. France did not move in yet, but it did convince the other European nations to recognize its "rights" to Tunisia. In 1881 French troops occupied the country and established a "protectorate" in which France took over the government's finances. Completing its conquest of Tunisia, France assumed control of its administration in 1883. Its hold on Algeria and Tunisia, combined with its expanding operations in West Africa, gave France a vast empire in northwest Africa by the 1880s.

Tripoli, the Ottoman Empire province that would form the basis of modern Libya, escaped European colonization during the 19th century. According to the same sort of agreement that gave France authority in Tunisia, Tripoli fell into Italy's "sphere of influence." The Italians did not pursue colonization there until 1911, but the French stayed out. Farther east, however, France and Britain battled for superiority in Egypt. Although Egypt was still nominally a province of the Ottoman Empire, the Ottomans had all but lost their grip on the territory. Both France and Britain, the world's two strongest international powers at the time, wanted Egypt for their own. The strategically located crossroads of Africa, Asia and Europe, where the vitally important Suez Canal opened in 1869, offered rich rewards to the nation that controlled it.

In 1876 burdensome international debt forced the Egyptian government to appoint British and French representatives to a commission charged with salvaging the country's finances. By 1879 British and French officials headed all the ministries of the Egyptian administration. The increasing involvement of foreigners—and non-Muslims, at that—in Egypt's internal affairs upset many Egyptians. A faction of the military tried to reassert Egyptian control in 1881, launching an armed uprising. France, distracted by its own domestic problems, could not divert resources to the problem, but the British responded forcefully, bombarding Alexandria and crushing the revolt in 1882. Despite French protests, Britain took over the government of Egypt, although it would not formally declare Egypt a protectorate until 1914.

From Egypt, Britain kept its eye on the upper Nile and the eastern Sudan, where modern Sudan now stands. The area was home to the Mahdists, Muslim fundamentalists whom Britain believed were too strong to be subjugated. In 1885 the British sent General Charles Gordon to the Egyptian-controlled city of Khartoum, deep in Mahdist territory, to hand it over to local rulers. But Gordon made a series of pompous diplomatic blunders that angered the Mahdists. Their forces attacked Khartoum and killed the general, who for some reason became a hero in England. The Mahdists established an independent state that lasted until 1898.

The French, meanwhile, had not abandoned their hopes for an empire that spanned all of North Africa. In 1897 they marched north

British and Mahdist forces fighting at the battle of Khartoum, 1885. (Picture Collection, The Branch Libraries, The New York Public Library)

and east from a base on the Congo River, reaching the upper White Nile in 1898. But the British had been alerted to the French threat and met their rivals with a larger, stronger force. The French retreated while the British inaugurated a campaign to take the Sudan from the Mahdists. They finally defeated the Mahdists in a bloody battle near Khartoum. The British now controlled all of northeast Africa.

THE WHITE PRESENCE IN EAST AFRICA

For much of the 19th century, Europeans had courted the friendship of the independent, Christian kingdom of Ethiopia. With the Ethiopians' permission, during the second half of the century, private European companies set up trading centers along the Indian Ocean coast near present-day Djibouti. The Ethiopians profited from trade with the Europeans as well as from rivalries among the whites, who tried to outdo each other in winning Ethiopian favor. In this way, Ethiopia acquired a large arsenal of firearms, which came in handy when their white "friends" challenged Ethiopian independence. France and Italy were the two major nations jostling for influence in the Horn of Africa in the 1880s. In 1884 France established French Somaliland in the area now occupied by Somalia. This move aroused no serious resistance, as the region was sparsely populated, but the British set up their own small protectorate around Djibouti. With Ethiopian agreement, the French also started constructing a railroad between their port at Obock and the new Ethiopian capital of Addis Ababa.

In 1883 the Italian government took over private Italian interests in northeast Africa and began expanding throughout Eritrea, which later became part of Ethiopia. They established a protectorate and signed a treaty of friendship with Ethiopia in 1889, but then claimed the treaty established an Italian protectorate over Ethiopia. Invading in the 1890s, the Italians met stiff resistance from highly trained, well-armed Ethiopian forces. The showdown came in 1896 at the battle of Adowa, where Ethiopian troops under Emperor Menelik II routed the Italian army. The victory secured Ethiopian independence and enhanced its international prestige while humiliating Italy.

South of Ethiopia and the Sudan, Britain and Germany competed for influence. In 1885 Germany declared the formation of German East Africa in the territory now known as Tanganyika. Britain had its own claims to the area, through its alliance with the sultan of Zanzibar, so between 1886 and 1890 the two nations negotiated the boundaries of the land to be claimed by each. They agreed that Britain would keep Zanzibar and take the area now occupied by Kenya and Uganda, and Germany would keep German East Africa. Neither seemed to consider the concerns of the Africans who had occupied these lands for centuries.

As soon as the agreement with Britain was signed, Germany leased a long strip of coastal land from the sultan of Zanzibar, whom Europeans recognized as having dominion over the area. A private German company took on administration of the region in order to minimize costs to the German government. But the company forced the Swahili, Arabs and Yao living there to work under conditions of virtual slavery and taxed them heavily, provoking a revolt in 1888. The German government stepped in to put down the rebellion and, after defeating the Africans in 1889, assumed direct control of German East Africa in 1890. In the interior, African resistance continued. Local peoples launched highly effective guerrilla attacks against German patrols and trading caravans, seriously compromising the profitability of German operations. One of the most powerful fighting forces in the area, the Masai, were debilitated by a plague that wiped out the herd of cattle upon which their culture was based. Germany managed to crush most of the other uprisings by 1898, but it was not until 1899 that the resilient Yao were subjugated.

The Africans of the new British territories to the north battled their invaders just as persistently. Like the Germans, Britain originally assigned administration of British East Africa (Kenya) and Uganda (so named for the mighty Buganda people of Lake Victoria) to a private trading company, the Imperial British East Africa Company. Hoping to avoid war with the Buganda, who had earlier converted to Christianity, the company persuaded them to accept British overrule. The Bunyoro were not so amenable, though, and used guerrilla tactics against the whites starting in 1894. The British government took over from the company that year and defeated the Bunyoro by 1898. In Kenya, where the stricken Masai could offer little resistance, the company was removed in 1895 and the British quickly suppressed a revolt by coastal Swahili. Omani Arabs from Zanzibar were installed as local rulers under the British.

The British also maintained an interest in the land south of German East Africa, in the vicinity of Lake Malawi. Earlier in the century British missionaries had established quasi-colonial authority over the ancestral homeland of the Maravi people, an authority the British government intended to expand. In 1883 a British consul arrived over the objections of the Portuguese, who had laid claim to Mozambique for centuries. Nevertheless, Britain proclaimed the establishment of the Central African Protectorate in 1889. Two years later, a treaty between the rival Europeans granted the area east of Lake Malawi to the Portuguese and that west of the lake to the British.

Mozambique was torn apart by African rebellions for the next 20 years. An 1894 attack by Africans on the Portuguese authorities was short-lived, but the prazeros, settlers of mixed African and Portuguese descent, proved harder to control. The Portuguese formed an army of Portuguese and African soldiers to collect taxes and enforce order in the interior, but it was 1901 before they achieved control over most of their holdings; resistance from the Yao was not extinguished until 1912. Likewise, the British encountered violent resistance in the Central African Protectorate (renamed Nyasaland in 1897) throughout the 1890s. Heavy taxation and brutal treatment at British hands inspired repeated risings among the Yao, the Swahili, the Chewa, the Ngoni and the Maravi. Many among the proud Maravi committed suicide rather than submit to British rule, but by the turn of the century the British had put an end to organized rebellion.

During the 1890s the southernmost portions of East Africa also fell under white control. There, on the land now occupied by Zambia and Zimbabwe, the white invader was the British South Africa Company, founded in 1889 by Cape Colony tycoon Cecil Rhodes. Rhodes, who made his fortune mining diamonds and gold in southern Africa, wanted to find the ancient gold mines of Great Zimbabwe, rumored to lie in Changamire/Mutapa territory. In 1888 he signed a fraudulent treaty with the Ndebele, who controlled the area, to gain access to the mines. The Ndebele believed they were signing a treaty of friendship and that their empire would remain undisturbed by whites.

But in 1890, with the approval of the British government, Rhodes' company sent a "pioneer column" of white settlers into the area dubbed Southern Rhodesia (Zimbabwe) to set up farms and search for the mines. The mines they found had little gold left in them. Dismayed, the settlers looted ancient sites, forever destroying pieces of African history. When the Ndebele tried to protest in 1893, Rhodes sent troops in to take their land and cattle. The Ndebele joined with the Shona (descendants of Great Zimbabwe) in a massive uprising in 1896 and almost succeeded in ejecting Rhodes' company, but with assistance from Cape Colony, Rhodes brought the bloody rebellion to an end in 1897. He then swept into "Northern Rhodesia" (Zambia) to claim that region for Britain. There the Bemba put up a tough fight until 1898, when a French Catholic missionary seized the throne and accepted British rule.

THE SCRAMBLE FOR WEST AFRICA

European competition for African colonies was perhaps most cut-throat in West Africa, a region with rich resources and a highly developed trading system. The British and French had established solid presences and a few colonial outposts there by 1870 and competed fiercely for territory. West Africa's fate was sealed in 1884 and 1885 at the Berlin West Africa Conference. After proclaiming protectorates over Togo, Cameroon and South-West Africa (Namibia), Germany invited the other Europeans to a summit to negotiate the continuation of free trade along the Niger and Congo rivers. But the conference went much further, laying the ground rules for the European recognition of colonies in West Africa. The participants agreed to respect each others' claims to territory whenever the claimant had already "effectively occupied" the area by setting up missionary stations and trading posts.

Pushing eastward into the continent from its holdings along the Senegal, France worked to extend its grip over all West Africa. Their first move, in 1879, was to begin construction of a railroad from the port of Dakar in Senegal to a point on the upper Niger River, thereby diverting trade to their merchants. In 1882 they cast their net even wider, proclaiming protectorates on the northern bank of the lower Congo (French Congo, now Gabon) and at Porto Novo (now Benin). Porto Novo was particularly important to France because it was located between two British domains, thereby breaking Britain's monopolistic control over the Gold Coast. During the late 1880s the French also extended their holdings along the Congo, declaring the formation of Moyen (middle) Congo (now Kongo) and Ubangi-Chari (now Central African Republic).

As they pushed toward the Niger, the French first encountered the Tukolor. They signed a treaty promising not to invade Tukolor territory but broke it in 1883. Continuing French pressure and Tukolor resistance produced a second treaty in 1887, but the French broke that one as well. Fighting broke out and the French obliterated numerous Tukolor towns using advanced artillery. They finally subdued the Tukolor in 1893. Senegalese soldiers commanded by French officers clashed with Mandinka warriors throughout the 1880s. France signed a treaty with the Mandinka in 1886 and then broke it in 1887, at the same time civil war broke out among the Mandinka. When the French invaded from the north in 1891, the Mandinka defended themselves by burning their fields and villages. The French withdrew and the Mandinka moved to new land to the east. Seeking protection against the French, the Mandinka signed a treaty with the British in 1890. But the British recognized French claims to Mandinka territory, and the French returned just as famine struck. The Mandinka fell in 1898.

France marched farther into the Sudan, reaching Borno territory just as that culture was in the throes of a civil war. Easily exploiting the situation to their own advantage, the French conquered the area in 1900. During the 1890s they asserted their dominion over Porto Novo, conquering the Dahomey by 1894. To the west, between independent Liberia and Britain's Gold Coast protectorate, the French claimed present-day Ivory Coast as a colony in 1893. The many small states of the region would fight the French for 20 years before white dominance was assured, but by 1900 France had succeeded in building a huge West African colony. Stretching from Senegal in the west to the border of British Sudan in the east, and with few interruptions from Algeria (also French-controlled) in the north to the Congo River in the south, French West Africa was a formidable conquest.

The British also pursued colonies in West Africa, struggling to defend and expand their possessions in the face of French rapacity. In 1874 they fought the Asante for control of trade on the Gold Coast. After defeating them, the British forced the Asante to sign a treaty giving various trade concessions, but they did not assume direct rule over Asante territory. While Britain continued trading, the Asante rebuilt their forces. In the 1890s they began asserting their rights. Britain invaded Asante territory again in 1895–96 and subdued them without a battle, declaring a protectorate over most of modern Ghana. In 1901 Britain annexed the colony of Gold Coast.

After the Berlin Conference of 1884–85, Britain built on its colony at Lagos and declared a protectorate in the Niger River delta, naming it the Oil Rivers Protectorate. The government granted a charter to the Royal Niger Company to govern the area and trade in palm oil, the delta's main export. As Britain's official interest in the lower Niger River expanded, the government replaced the company as administrator and launched a push into the interior. Between 1892 and 1902 the British extended their rule over most of the region that makes up modern Nigeria. They used African troops to conquer the peoples of the area, including the Yoruba, the Sokoto and numerous small forest states. The fighting did not stop until 1910, by which time the British called their colony Nigeria.

The Congo River basin holdings claimed by King Leopold II of Belgium in 1878 were formally recognized by the Berlin conference; the king declared the Congo Free State in 1885. The king's personal empire, not subject to the laws of Belgium or any other European nation, the Congo Free State was anything but free for its African inhabitants. Leopold leased the land to concessionary companies that agreed to build railroads and cut the king in on a share of their profits. These companies extracted their profits cruelly, forcing Africans to work for them and killing those who wouldn't. The commodity they sought was rubber, which was in rapidly increasing demand in Europe for bicycle and automobile tires. Africans of the region, especially Swahili traders and merchants such as Tippu Tip in the east, rejected the whites' oppressive rule. But Leopold's army, the *Force Publique*, was ruthless and well armed; fighting continued for the rest of the century. In 1908 Leopold turned over his expensive venture to Belgium, which renamed it Belgian Congo.

To the south, meanwhile, Portugal exploited African rivalries in Angola to extend its influence over a large area. The rubber boom that fueled white activity in Congo Free State also brought profits to Angola. This prosperity allowed the Africans of the region to buy guns with which to resist the Portuguese. It was 1912 before the Portuguese conquered the last of the rebels in Angola. On Angola's western edge, the Lozi of the upper Zambezi sought British protection, mostly against raids by neighboring Africans. The Lozi signed a treaty with Cecil Rhodes in 1889, but Rhodes offered no material assistance to them until 1893. Still, the Lozi entered the colonial era without losing much of their land or any of their blood.

THE MINERAL REVOLUTION IN SOUTHERN AFRICA

Aside from Germany's claim on South-West Africa (modern Namibia), southern Africa escaped "the scramble" typical of the rest of Africa at the end of the 1800s. Instead, the era was one of consolidation of existing European claims and development of European activity. Chief among these activities was mining, for diamonds were discovered in Griqua territory in 1867 and gold was found in Transvaal in 1886.

As soon as diamonds were discovered, people rushed to Kimberly, the town nearest the first diamond field, from all over southern Africa. A city of 30,000 arose almost overnight. White diggers staked their claims and employed migrant black laborers to extract the gems from the earth. Before long, surface deposits had been exhausted and the miners had to dig deeper. As deep mining was expensive, small miners could no longer participate. Diamond mining became the pursuit of a few large companies, led by the De Beers Company founded by Cecil Rhodes. De Beers gradually bought out all its rivals and employed large numbers of poorly paid blacks. But even though their wages were low, migrant Africans who worked the mines made more than they could have made elsewhere and often used their pay to buy guns.

The diamond rush renewed conflicts over land. As whites tried to claim more land—where they might find more diamonds—newly armed blacks put up a fight. During the seventh Frontier War (1876), many Boers were forced off their land. The eighth Frontier War of 1877–78 pitted the British against the Xhosa and left the Xhosa with only a small "reserve" to live on. In 1879, in the ninth and final Frontier War, the British went up against the Zulu, at first suffering a humiliating defeat but then smashing the warrior kingdom. Part of Zulu territory was annexed to Transvaal and the rest became a British colony in 1887. Meanwhile, seeking to block Boer and German expansion, which threatened to cut off Cape Colony's overland route to the rest of Africa, the British established the protectorate of Bechuanaland (Botswana) in 1885.

In 1871 Britain annexed Griqualand, the source of diamonds, to Cape Colony; in 1872 it granted the colony self-government. The Boers resented the British annexation of the diamond mines but were powerless to do anything about it. Indeed, in 1877 Britain annexed Transvaal, which had gone bankrupt. Boer resistance was so relentless, however, that Britain granted Transvaal its independence again in 1881, a move it would soon regret. Five years later gold was discovered near Pretoria, the capital of Transvaal. The gold mines soon outstripped the diamond mines as southern Africa's major source of wealth. Abundant coal in the area allowed for rapid industrialization, and the newly founded city of Johannesburg soon became the largest city in sub-Saharan Africa.

Gold mining in Transvaal required large infusions of capital, which the Boers could not provide. Foreign investors, especially the British (such as Cecil Rhodes), controlled the mining interests, although the Boers retained a grip on the supporting industries that thrived alongside. The government of Transvaal also taxed the mining operations heavily, growing rich on the revenues. The Transvaal Boers developed a strong army that steadily expanded Boer holdings into areas still ruled by Africans. They hoped to make themselves impervious to the British, whose policies they had long loathed.

When Cecil Rhodes became prime minister of Cape Colony in 1890, he decided to check the growth of Boer power. In 1895 he tried to foment a rebellion of miners in the Boer republic, but his plan failed and only heightened tensions between the British and the Boers. Rhodes was forced to resign in 1896. Britain soon demanded government reform in Transvaal aimed at improving conditions for British business there, but the Boers refused. When British troops massed at the Transvaal border in 1899, the Boers declared war. The bloody Anglo-Boer War lasted until 1902, when Britain defeated the Boers and reduced the two Boer republics to the status of British colonies. In 1909, these colonies were joined into the independent Union of South Africa, now known as the Republic of South Africa. Basutoland (Lesotho), Bechuanaland and Swaziland became territories regulated by Britain.

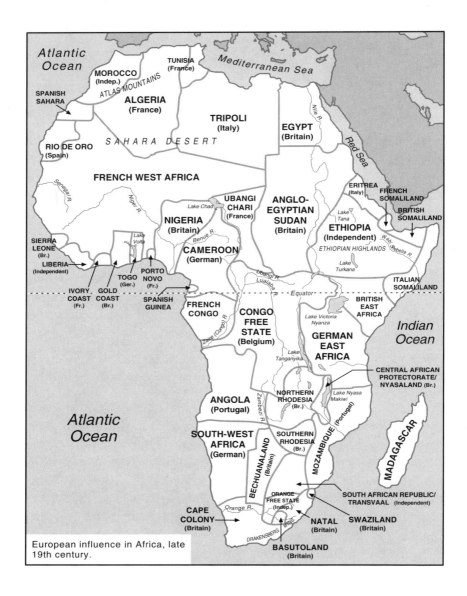

Atlantic
Ocean

MOROCCO
(Indep.)

SPANISH
SAHARA

ATLAS MOUNTAINS

ALGERIA
(France)

TUNISIA
(France)

Mediterranean Sea

TRIPOLI
(Italy)

EGYPT
(Britain)

RIO DE ORO
(Spain)

SAHARA DESERT

Red Sea

Nile R.

Senegal R.

Niger R.

FRENCH WEST AFRICA

UBANGI
CHARI
(France)

Lake Chad

NIGERIA
(Britain)

Benue R.

CAMEROON
(German)

ANGLO-
EGYPTIAN
SUDAN
(Britain)

ERITREA
(Italy)

FRENCH
SOMALILAND

BRITISH
SOMALILAND

Lake
Tana

ETHIOPIA
(Independent)

ETHIOPIAN HIGHLANDS

Webi

Shebelle R.

SIERRA
LEONE
(Br.)

Lake
Volta

LIBERIA
(Independent)

TOGO
(Ger.)

PORTO
NOVO
(Fr.)

IVORY
COAST
(Fr.)

GOLD
COAST
(Br.)

SPANISH
GUINEA

FRENCH
CONGO

Zaire (Congo) R.

CONGO
FREE
STATE
(Belgium)

Ubangi R.

Lualaba R.

Equator

Lake
Turkana

Lake Victoria
Nyanza

Lake
Tanganyika

ITALIAN
SOMALILAND

BRITISH
EAST
AFRICA

Indian
Ocean

GERMAN
EAST
AFRICA

CENTRAL AFRICAN
PROTECTORATE/
NYASALAND (Br.)

Atlantic
Ocean

ANGOLA
(Portugal)

Zambezi R.

NORTHERN
RHODESIA
(Br.)

Lake Nyasa
Makiwi

MOZAMBIQUE (Portugal)

MADAGASCAR

SOUTH-WEST
AFRICA
(German)

BECHUANALAND
(Britain)

SOUTHERN
RHODESIA
(Br.)

ORANGE
FREE STATE
(Indep.)

SOUTH AFRICAN REPUBLIC/
TRANSVAAL (Independent)

CAPE
COLONY
(Britain)

Orange R.

DRAKENSBERG

VAAL R.

NATAL
(Britain)

BASUTOLAND
(Britain)

SWAZILAND
(Britain)

European influence in Africa, late
19th century.

By the close of the 19th century, many Europeans had settled in
Africa—not only in southern Africa, where they had lived in large
numbers since the 1600s, but in the new colonies, especially Kenya,
Southern Rhodesia and Namibia. More important to indigenous
Africans, however, were the spread of firearms, Christianity, anti-

W. E. B. DuBOIS ON AFRICA

African-American writer and teacher W. E. B. DuBois (1868–1963) observed the white colonization of Africa and wrote angrily of its impact on African culture. This excerpt comes from his book *The World and Africa*:

> There came to Africa an end of industry, especially industry guided by taste and art. Cheap European goods pushed in and threw the native products out of competition. Rum and gin displaced the milder native drinks. The beautiful patterned cloth, brocades and velvets disappeared before their cheap imitations in Manchester [England] calicos. Methods of work were lost and forgotten.
>
> With all this went the fall and disruption of the family, the deliberate attack upon the ancient African clan by missionaries. The invading investors who wanted cheap labor at the gold mines, the diamond mines, the copper and tin mines, the oil forests and cocoa fields, followed the missionaries. The authority of the family was broken up; the authority and tradition of the clan disappeared; the power of the chief was transmuted into the rule of the white district commissioner. The old religion was held up to ridicule, the old culture and ethical standards were degraded or disappeared, and gradually all over Africa spread the inferiority complex, the fear of color, the worship of white skin, the imitation of white ways of doing and thinking, whether good, bad, or indifferent. By the end of the 19th century the degradation of Africa was as complete as organized human means could make it. Chieftains, representing a thousand years of striving human culture, were decked out in second-hand London top hats, while Europe snickered.

slavery sentiment, industrialism, cash-based trade and racism. These, along with the imposition of European laws on African societies, had a profound impact on African culture. Most colonial powers did not develop a coherent colonial policy until after the era of the scramble, when they began to confront the task of governing a continent. In some colonies Africans were left to themselves on a day-to-day basis; in others, European rule had direct, and usually harmful, results on ordinary Africans. But whatever the case, by 1900 most Africans had lost the freedom to govern themselves, to control their economic lives and, often, to pursue their religious and cultural traditions. Under colonialism, Africa entered its own Dark Ages, from which it would not emerge until well into in the 20th century. When it did, the scars of white domination would not heal quickly. Some would never heal at all.

CHRONOLOGY

1415 • The Portuguese capture the Moroccan port of Ceuta.

1482 • The Portuguese build their first fort in Africa, at Elmina on the Gold Coast.

1488 • Portuguese explorers become the first Europeans to round the southern tip of Africa.

1490 • The Ethiopian court receives its first European visitors, the Portuguese.

1500s • The Funj Sultanate rises along the middle Nile.

• The independent kingdom of Morocco unifies under the Sa'dids.

• The Oromo migrate into Ethiopian territory.

• The Maravi resist Portuguese invasion.

• Borno-Kanem extends its influence in the western Sudan.

1505 • The Portuguese attack the city-states of the east coast.

1506 • Afonso I, a Kongolese convert to Christianity, seizes the throne of Kongo.

1517 • The Ottomans of Turkey invade Egypt.

1526 • Adal invades Ethiopia.

1532 • The Portuguese ship the first African slaves to the Americas.

1543	•	Ethiopia expels Adal with the help of the Portuguese.
1560s–70s	•	East Africans of the interior repel Portuguese invasions.
1568	•	The Jaga conquer Kongo.
1571	•	The Mutapa repel a Portuguese invasion.
1574	•	The Portuguese help Kongo eliminate the Jaga.
1575	•	The Portuguese settle at Luanda in Angola.
1576	•	Africans destroy the Portuguese fort at Accra on the Gold Coast.
1580s	•	Civil war breaks out in Songhai.
	•	The Ndongo resist a Portuguese invasion.
1591	•	Morocco conquers Songhai.
1599	•	The Portuguese extinguish the last resistance among Swahili city-states of the east coast.
1600s	•	The Yoruba kingdom of Oyo expands from its base in the interior to the Atlantic coast.
	•	The kingdom of Kongo collapses.
	•	The kingdom of Kasanje forms in west-central Africa.
	•	The Lozi unite under a single king.
1603	•	Morocco abandons Songhai.
1610	•	The Dutch end the Portuguese monopoly on African trade.
1623	•	The Maravi penetrate Mutapa territory.
1637–42	•	The Dutch East India Company takes possession of Portuguese forts on the west coast.
1648	•	Ethiopia expels the Jesuit missionaries.
1650	•	Dahomey organizes as a centralized state.
1652	•	The Dutch East India Company establishes a provisioning station on the Cape of Good Hope.
1659–60	•	The Khoikhoi rise against Dutch settlers near Cape Town.
1670s	•	The Akan peoples unite into the kingdom of Asante.

1673–77	•	The Khoi-Dutch war expands Dutch holdings in southern Africa.
1680–96	•	Changamire conquers Torwa and Mutapa.
1698	•	Mombasa passes from Portuguese to Omani control.
1700s	•	Ethiopia establishes its capital at Gondar.
	•	The Nyamwezi become the major power southeast of Lake Victoria.
	•	Civil war erupts in Benin.
	•	More than 6 million Africans are exported to the Americas as slaves.
	•	Boers expand into Khoikhoi and San territory.
1700s–1800s	•	The Fulani Muslims of the Sokoto empire wage a series of jihads to expand their territory.
1700	•	The British and French break the Dutch monopoly on the slave trade.
1730	•	The Yoruba state of Oyo conquers Dahomey.
1750	•	The Futa Jalon fall to the Fulani.
1750–1800	•	The British dominate the slave trade.
1776	•	The Futa Toro fall to the Fulani.
1779–81	•	The Boers fight the Xhosa in the first Frontier War.
1787	•	Sierra Leone is founded.
1788	•	The Association for the Discovery of the Interior Parts of Africa (the Africa Association) is founded in England.
1793	•	The second Frontier War is fought in southern Africa.
1795	•	The Dutch East India Company defeats a Boer rebellion against company authority. The British take control of the cape from the Dutch.
1795–97	•	Sponsored by the Africa Association, Englishman Mungo Park explores part of the Niger River, launching the age of European exploration.
1798	•	Under Napoleon Bonaparte, France ejects the Ottomans from Egypt.

1799 • Agents of the London Missionary Society arrive in southern Africa.

1800s • Egyptians and Swahili disrupt Nyamwezi trading.
 • Prazeros, Swahili and local peoples compete for control of the East African interior.
 • Oyo is conquered by the Fulani.
 • The Chokwe rise in western Africa.

1800 • The Buganda supplant the Bunyoro as the major power around Lake Victoria.

1800–03 • The third Frontier War is fought in southern Africa.

1800–16 • The three Nguni powers wage wars of expansion against each other.

1800–40 • The Nguni Mfecane and Sotho Difaqane take place: war, social upheaval and migration. The Ndebele state is formed on Tswana land.

1801 • Britain helps the Ottomans regain power in Egypt.

1803 • The British return their southern African holdings to the Dutch.

1804 • The Church Missionary Society begins its work in Sierra Leone.

1804–17 • The European nations ban the West African slave trade.

1805–06 • Mungo Park makes his second expedition along the Niger.

1806 • Muhammad Ali becomes pasha of Egypt and begins a program of modernization.
 • The British retake the cape from the Dutch.

1808 • The last Hausa city-state falls to the Fulani.
 • Britain declares Sierra Leone a crown colony.

1811 • The Wesleyan Methodist Missionary Society sets up a base in Sierra Leone.

1811–12 • The fourth Frontier War is fought in southern Africa.

1815 • The British import 5,000 settlers to Cape Colony.

1816 • Drought in Nguni territory exacerbates political tensions; Shaka becomes chief of the Zulu.

1818 • Masina is founded on the upper Niger River.
  • Dahomey declares its independence from Oyo.
  • The Nguni state of Ndwandwe executes Dingiswayo, the leader of the Nguni state of Mthwetha; Shaka, chief of the Zulu, replaces him.

1818–19 • The fifth Frontier War is fought in southern Africa.

1820s • The Zulu force their rivals out of Nguni territory and form the Zulu kingdom.

1821 • Egypt crushes the Funj Sultanate.
  • Moshoeshoe organizes the kingdom of Basotho.

1822 • Free blacks from the United States settle Liberia.

1822–37 • Omani Arabs take over the ports of the east coast; Zanzibar becomes the capital of the Omani empire.

1827 • Fourah Bay College, the first African university, is founded in Sierra Leone.

1828 • Two of Shaka's half-brothers assassinate the Zulu leader.

1830s • The Nguni of southern Africa migrate into East Africa, where they are called the Ngoni.
  • The Kololo conquer the Lozi.
  • Nguni displaced by Zulu wars form the Swazi state.

1830s–40s • Peak years of the East African slave trade.

1830 • Englishmen John and Richard Lander find the mouth of the Niger River.
  • France takes Algiers.

1833 • Cape Colony frees all slaves within its borders.

1834–35 • The sixth Frontier War is fought in southern Africa.

1837 • The Boer "Great Trek" begins.

1838–39 • The Zulus resist Boer expansion but are defeated.

1840s–60s • Tukolor expands along the upper Niger River.

1840 • The British establish a consulate at Zanzibar.

1843	•	Basotho signs a treaty with Britain for protection against the Boers.
	•	Britain annexes the colony of Natal.
1847	•	Liberia declares its independence from the United States.
1848	•	France annexes Algeria.
1850s	•	The British build a network of railroads in Egypt.
1850	•	Quinine is discovered to cure malaria.
	•	The Africa Association renames itself the Royal Geographical Society.
1852	•	Britain recognizes the independent Boer state, South African Republic (Transvaal).
1852–56	•	English missionary David Livingstone crosses the continent from Luanda to Mozambique.
1853	•	Britain grants Cape Colony a constitution.
1854	•	Britain recognizes the independent Boer state, Orange Free State.
1855	•	Tewodros II becomes emperor of Ethiopia.
1856–59	•	Richard Burton and John Speke explore the Nile River and Lake Tanganyika.
1857	•	The British start launching regular steamship missions up the Niger River.
	•	The French occupy Cape Verde (Dakar).
1857–61	•	Tunis establishes a constitutional government.
1858–64	•	Livingstone charts the Zambezi River, names Victoria Falls and reaches Lake Malawi.
1861	•	The British annex Lagos as a crown colony.
1862–64	•	Speke and James Grant reach Lake Victoria, the source of the Nile River.
1864	•	The Lozi force the Kololo from their territory.
1865–90s	•	The Mandinka empire dominates the western Sudan south of Tukolor.
1867	•	Diamonds are discovered in Griqua territory.

1868 • The British depose Ethiopia's Tewodros II.

1869 • The Suez Canal opens in Egypt.

1870s • The British launch steamship trade on the lakes and rivers of East Africa.

1870s–80s • Tippu Tip heads a powerful trading empire along the upper Congo River.

1870 • The Boer expansion ends.

1871 • Britain annexes Basotho and Griqualand to Cape Colony.

1872 • Britain grants self-rule to Cape Colony.

1873 • The East African slave trade is outlawed.

1874–77 • Henry Morton Stanley charts the Congo River.

1876 • The seventh Frontier War is fought in southern Africa.

1877 • The British annex Transvaal.

1877–78 • The eighth Frontier War is fought in southern Africa.

1879 • France eradicates the last resistance to its rule in Algeria.

• The ninth Frontier War is fought in southern Africa.

1880s • The slave trade comes to an end.

1881 • France declares a protectorate in Tunisia.

• The British grant Transvaal its independence.

1882 • Britain takes control of Egypt.

• France proclaims protectorates in French Congo and Porto Novo.

1884 • France establishes French Somaliland.

• Germany proclaims protectorates in Togo, Cameroon and South-West Africa.

1884–85 • The European nations negotiate aspects of the colonial partition at the Berlin West Africa Conference.

1885 • Fundamentalist Muslims establish the Mahdist Sudan.

• Germany claims German East Africa.

• Britain sets up the Oil Rivers Protectorate.

- Belgian King Leopold II declares the Congo Free State.
- Britain establishes the Bechuanaland protectorate.

late 1880s
- France establishes Moyen Congo and Ubangi-Chari.

1886
- Britain claims Kenya.
- Gold is discovered in Transvaal.

1889
- Britain proclaims the Central African Protectorate (Nyasaland).

1890
- The British South African Company sends white settlers into territory they name Southern Rhodesia.

1891
- Portugal and Britain sign a treaty granting Mozambique to the Portuguese.

1893
- France completes the expansion of French West Africa.

1894
- Britain establishes a protectorate in Uganda.

1895–96
- Britain establishes a protectorate in the Gold Coast.

1896
- Ethiopia crushes Italian invaders at the battle of Adowa.

1897
- Cecil Rhodes claims Southern Rhodesia for Britain.

1898
- The British conquer the Mahdist Sudan.

1899–1902
- The Anglo-Boer War reduces Transvaal and Orange Free State to British colonies.

FURTHER READING

NON-FICTION BOOKS

Bascom, William. *African Art in Cultural Perspective* (New York: W. W. Norton & Company, 1973). Concise, illustrated overview of African art.

Davidson, Basil. *Africa in History* (New York: Macmillan, 1968). Solid, well-written history by one of the leading authorities on Africa.

———. *The African Slave Trade* (Boston: Little, Brown, 1961). Engaging narrative of the slave trade from the African perspective.

Denoon, Donald, and Balam Nyeko. *Southern Africa Since 1800* (Essex, England: Longman Group, 1972). Thorough but dense history of 19th-century southern Africa.

DuBois, W. E. B. *The World and Africa* (New York: International Publishers, 1965). A look at African history through the eyes of the respected African-American writer and educator; excellent despite some difficult language.

Fage, J. D. *A History of Africa*, 2d ed. (London: Unwin Hyman Ltd., 1988). Broad, comprehensive history of the continent; academic tone; assumes some prior knowledge.

Harris, Joseph E. *Africans and Their History* (New York: New American Library, 1987). Readable history of the continent from the African perspective.

Jackson, John G. *Introduction to African Civilizations* (New York: Carol Publishing Group, 1990). Reprint of a 1940s book on the impact of African civilizations on the rest of the world. Dated language but easy to read.

Oliver, Roland, and Anthony Atmore. *Africa Since 1800* (Cambridge, England: Cambridge University Press, 1981). Complete recent history of the continent; fairly accessible.

Oliver, Roland, and J. D. Fage. *A Short History of Africa* (London: The Penguin Group, 1990). Compact, sometimes difficult overview; highly recommended.

Shillington, Kevin. *History of Africa* (London: Macmillan Publishers, 1989). Excellent illustrated textbook on the topic; ideal for young adults.

Thompson, Robert Farris. *Flash of the Spirit: Afro-American Art and Philosophy* (New York: Random House, 1983). Fascinating, entertaining look at the impact of African art, music and religion in the Americas; valuable background on Africa; illustrated.

FICTION BOOKS

Forbath, Peter. *The Last Hero* (New York: Simon & Schuster, 1988). Accessible, historically accurate novel about the role of explorer H. M. Stanley in the British conquest of the Sudan.

Matthee, Dalene. *Fiela's Child* (New York: Alfred A. Knopf, 1986). Novel about African and Boer life in southern Africa during the late 19th century; ideal for young adults.

INDEX

Boldface numbers indicate special treatment of topic. *Italic* numbers indicate illustrations and captions. Numbers followed by "*m*" indicate maps.

abolitionism 22, 85–88
Abomey 47
Accra 70
Adal *27m*, 28, 73
Addis Ababa 116
Admad, Muhammad (the Madhi) 19
Adowa, Battle of 30, 116
Afonso I 52, 70–71
Africa Association 108–109
African-Americans 86–87
Afrikaners *See* Boers
age-set structure 31, 51, 60, 62
agriculture: ancient cultures 4–6, *5*; East Africa 26, 31–33; New World 70, 74, 76–78, 80, 85, 88; nomads 24, 57; North Africa 9–10, 18, 20, 22, 29; southern Africa 59–61, 63, 90–95, 97–98; West Africa 44, 48, 51–53, 70, 82–84, 86, 102
Akan 46
Aksum 6
alafins 48
Alawids 24
Alexander the Great 6
Alexandria 104, 115
Algeria *13m*, 19–22, 77, **105**, 113, 120, *124m*
Algiers 20–22, *22*, 105, 113
Ali, Muhammad 18–19
Allah 16–17
al-Maghrib **19–22**
Al-Mansur, Ahmad 23
Almohads 8
Almoravids 8
American Colonization Society 87
Anglo-Boer War 123
Angola 41, 79, 86, 109, 121–122, *124m*
animism 50
Ankole *27m*, 31–33
Anti-Slavery Squadron 86–88
apartheid 85, 89–98, 125
Arabia 77, 88
Arabs 1, 7–8, 12, 14, 19–22, 37, 39, 77, 117
architecture 4, 35, 50
Arma *41m*, 43
art 8–9, 15, 40–41, 43, 46, 48–49, **50**, 57, 60, 84–85, 125
artillery 112, 120
Asante (Ashanti) *41m*, 46–47, 102, 107, 120–121
assagai (spear) 62
Atlas Mountains *13m*, *124m*
Azores 10

bananas 33, 51

Bantu 28, 55, 57–59
barkcloth 33
Barth, Henry 109
Basotho *56m*, 65, 66, 98
Basutoland (Lesotho) *56m*, 66, 123, *124m*
Batlokwa (Tlokwa) *56m*, 66
Baule 46
Bechuanaland (Botswana) 123, *124m*
bedouins 24
Belgian Congo *See* Congo Free State
Belgium 121, *124m*
Bemba *27m*, 36, 119
Benin *See* Porto Novo
Berbers 7–8, *13m*, 21–25
Berlin West Africa Conference (1884-85) 119, 121
bey 21
Bisa *27m*, 36
Boers (Afrikaners) **90–98**; Anglo-Boer War 123; attitudes toward Africans 90, 94, 96; expansion 59, 62, 64, 66, 90–98, 92; missionaries 107; raids against 65, 122–123
Boer War 123
Borno 20, *41m*, 42–44, 120
Botswana *See* Bechuanaland
brass 48
Britain *See* Great Britain
British East Africa 117, *124m*
British Somaliland *124m*
British South Africa Company 118
bronze 48
Bruce, James 108
Buganda *27m*, 31–33, *34*, 109, 117
Bunyoro *27m*, 31–33, 117
Burton, Richard 109
Burundi *27m*, 33

Cairo 18, 104
calendars 4
Cameroon 107, 119, *124m*
Canary Islands 2
Cape Colony 94–98, 109, 123, *124m*
Cape of Good Hope 68, 74, 89–90, *91*
Cape Town 90–94
Cape Verde (Dakar) 10, 102, 119
caravans 14, 33–37, 39, 54, 68, 117
Carthage 6
cassava 51, 53
cattle herding: ancient cultures 4, 6; East Africa 29, 30–31, 33, 35–36, 117; North Africa 9, 16, 24; southern Africa 10, 55, 57, 60, 65, 90–94; West Africa 44, 53
Central African Protectorate (Nyasaland) 118, *124m*
Central African Republic *See* Ubangi-Chari
Ceuta 10
Changamire *27m*, 35, 36, *56m*, 63, 75, 118
Charles X 105
Chewa 118
chiefdoms 33, 35–36, 46–47, 49, 52, 55, 60–62, 64, 83, 125

chikunda (soldiers) 37
Chokwe *41m*, 54
Christianity: conversion to 29, 52, 65, 70, 74, 82, 86–87, 100, 106–108, 117; Ethiopian 28–30, 72–73; introduction of 6, 100, 104–108, 124
Church Missionary Society 106
cities *See name of city*
city-states 26, **37–42**, 100 *See also* Hausa, Swahili
civil service 18
clans 21, 24–25, 31, 46, 60, 125
class structure 33, 54, 70, 77, 87, 93, 107
climate **2–3**, 14, 57, 59
cloth *See* textiles
coal 123
cocoa 101, 125
coffee 31, 33, 76, 80, 87, 101
colonialism **112–126**; East Africa 37, 71–74, 116–119; effects of 11, 50, 124–126; justification for 57, 85, 108, 111; North Africa 23–25, 103, 105, 113–116; southern Africa 90, 94–96, 107, 122; West Africa 43, 69–71, 87, 100–102, 107, 119–122
commerce *See* trade
concubines 77
Congo Free State (Belgian Congo) 38, 111, 121, *124m*
Congo River 2, 11, 30, *41m*, 51, 109–111, *110*, 116, 119–121
conversion, religious: to Christianity 29, 52, 65, 70, 74, 82, 86–87, 100, 104–108, 117; to Islam 7, 16, 29, 44–46
copper 31, 37, 48, 57, 70, 83, 125
Coptic Christianity 73
corn (maize) 51, 52, 61
corsairs *See* pirates
cotton 18, 31, 36, 49, 76, 80, 88
Covilha, Pero de 11
Creoles 86
cultural exchange 7, 14, 36, 37, 39, 60, 86, 106, 125
cultural identity 9, 28, 40, 84, 86–87, 107
cultural unity 14–15, 17, 63
customs *See name of culture*
Cyrenaica 6
Cyrene 6

Dahomey *41m*, 46–48, 107, 120
Dakar *See* Cape Verde
"Dark Continent" 3, 82, 99–100, 108
De Beers Company 122
debt, foreign 19, 22, 114
Denmark 78, 86, 100, 101
dey 21, 22
diamonds 98, 118, 122–123, 125
Difaqane 64–66, 96
Dingiswayo 62
diseases 52, 74, 93, 101, 109, 117
Djibouti 103, 116
dogs 57
Dominicans 74
dowry 60

Lake Malawi 109, 118
Lake Tanganyika 2, 109
Lake Turkana 29
Lake Victoria 2, 27m, 30–35, 109, 117
Lander, John and Richard 101
languages *See name of language*
leather 5, 14, 20, 23
"legitimate commerce" 24, 88, 100–104
Leopold II 111, 121
Lesotho (Basutoland) 56m, 66, 123, 124m
Liberia 41m, 46, **86–87**, 106, 124m
Libreville 106
Libya 114 *See also* Tripoli
liquor 71, 80, 90, 125
literacy 7, 15, 22, 45, 106
livestock *See* cattle, sheep
Livingstone, David 109
London Missionary Society 106
Lozi 41m, 53–54, 66, 122
Luanda 71, 109
Luba 10, 27m, 41m, 52–52
Lucy (hominid fossil) 3
Lunda 10, 52–53

machine gun 112
Madagascar 2, 27m, 56m, 91
Madeira 10
Madhi, the (Muhammad Admad) 19
Maghrib *See* al-Maghrib
Mahdists 13m, 19, 115–116
mais (rulers) 43
maize *See* corn
malaria 101, 109
Malawi *See* Maravi
Mali 8, 40
Malindi 72
Mamluks 8, 15–16
Mandinka 41m, 45–46, 82, 120
Manikongo 51
Mantatisi 66
manufacturing 44, 61, 82–84, 86, 99, 105, 112, 123, 125
marabouts (holy men) 21
Maravi (Malawi) 27m, 35–36, 118
marijuana 57
maritime trade 9, 12, 16, 20, 22, 26, 39, 68–71, 101
Masai 27m, 31, 32, 117
Masina 41m, 45
masks 9, 48, 50
Mauritius 75
Maxim gun 112
Mecca 16, 17
medicine 57
Mediterranean 3, 6, 8, 13m, 104
Menelik II 30, 116
Menes 4
mercantilism *See* trade
merchant-princes 83–85
Meroe 4–5
metals *See name of metal*
Mfecane 64–66, 96
migration 29, 31, 37, 53, 59, 92
military service: age-set 31, 60, 62; cavalry 48; forced labor 19, 37, 42; mercenaries 36, 70; reforms

15, 29–30, 43, 48, 62–64, 104; training 10, 29–30, 42, 52, 53, 62–63, 70, 73, 123; women 47, 63
millet 51, 60
minerals *See name of mineral*
mining: ancient cultures 8; colonization 113, 123; East Africa 31, 35–36; slave labor 77–78, 80, 83; southern Africa 118–119, 122–123; West Africa 70, 83
missionaries 29, 65, 70, 73, 74, 86, 95, 100, 104–108, 111, 118–119, 125
missionary schools 106, 107
missionary societies 106
molasses 87
Mombasa 27m, 39, 73, 75
Moors 7–8, 67
Morocco 10, 13m, **23–24**, 42–43, 77, 104, 113–114, 124m
Moshoeshoe **65**, 66, 98
Mt. Kenya 109
Mt. Kilimanjaro 109
Moyen Congo *See* Kongo
Mozambique 73, 82, 88, 91, 109, 118, 124m
Mthethwa 62
Muhammad (founder of Islam) 16–17
music 9, 47, 50, 107
Muslims 7–9, 12, 14–19, 21, 44, 67, 73, 77, 105, 115
Mutapa 10, 27m, 35–36, 56m, 74, 75, 118

Nakhti, tomb of 5
Nama 56m, 59
Namib desert 56m, 68
Namibia *See* South-West Africa
Napoleon Bonaparte 18
Napoleonic Wars 85
Natal 96–97, 124m
Ndebele 56m, 64–66, 118–119
Ndongo 10, 41m, 52–53, 71, 82
Ndwandwe *See* Ngoni
Netherlands, the 59, 75, 78–79, 86, 89, 90–94, 100, 101, 106
New World: demand for slaves 75, 76–79, 85, 88; European settlement 68, 74, 76, 78; triangular trade 61, 79–80, 85
Ngola 27m, 52
Ngoni (Ndwandwe) 37, 56m, 62–64, 118
Nguni 56m, 59–62, 64, 65
Ngwane 62–63, 64
Nigeria 82, 107, 121, 124m
Niger River 2, 8, 41m, 45, 101–102, 108–109, 119–121
Nile River 2–4, 13m, 16–17, 27m, 104, 109, 115
nobility 15, 77, 107
nomads 7–8, 13m, 18, 21–25, 41m, 44, 57, 59
North Africa 4–8, **12–25**, 13m, **113–116** *See also name of country, culture*
Northern Rhodesia (Zambia) 118–119, 124m

Nyamwezi 27m, 33
Nyasaland *See* Central African Protectorate

Obok 103, 116
Oil Rivers 101
Oil Rivers Protectorate 121
oils, aromatic 5, 20, 54, 87, 101, 121, 125
olive oil 20, 105
Omanis 38, 39, 75, 88, 117
oracles 51
Orange Free State 97, 124m
Oromo 27m, 29, 30
Ottomans 13m, 15–16, 18, 20–23, 27m, 72–73, 103, 114
Ovimbundu 41m, 54
Oyo 47–48

palm oil 54, 87, 101–102, 121
Park, Mungo 108
partition 112–126
pashas 15, 17
patriarchs 60
peanuts 101
Pemba 39
pepper *See* spices
Persia (Iran) 77
Phoenicians 1, 6
pirates and piracy 20–22, 24, 37, 105
plagues *See* diseases
plantains 33
polygamy 107
pombieros (slave agents) 81
Pondo 61
pope 11, 70, 73
population 29, 53–54, 61, 64, 82, 88
Porto Novo (Benin) 41m, 46, 49, 51, 69, 84, 107, 119–120, 124m
Portugal: colonization 20, 23, 28, 35–36, 39, 71–75, 118, 121–122, 124m; exploration 8–9, **10–11**, 68; trade 1, 36, 39, 52, 58–59, 69–75, 78, 89
pottery 10, 51, 58
prazeros 36–37, 74, 118
Pretoria 123
Príncipe *See* São Tomé and Príncipe
protectorates 113–116, 119
Protestants 106
pumpkins 60
Pygmies 51

quinine 101, 109

racism *See* apartheid
railroads 19, 104, 116, 119, 121
rain forests 3, 30, 41m, 46–51
rain making 60
Red Sea 16, 18, 104
refugees 64–66
religion *See also name of religion:* and art 46, 50; and government

63; and ritual 36, 50, 60, 86, 107, 125; and slave trade 84
Rhodes, Cecil 118–119, 122–123
Rio de Oro *124m*
Roman Catholic church 11, 70, 72–73, 106
Romans 1, 6
Royal Geographical Society 109
Royal Niger Company 113, 121
rozvi (soldiers) 36
rubber 54, 121
rum 71, 80, 125
Rwanda *27m*, 31, 33

Sa'dids 23
Sahara desert 1–3, *13m*, 14, **24–25**, 25, *41m*, 45, 68, 109, *124m*
Said bin Sultan, Seyyid 39
salt 14, 23, 31, 33, 35, 37, 42, 47, 70
San (Bushmen) 10, *56m*, 57, 59–60, 89–92, 106
Sanusi, Muhammad al- *13m*, 24, *41m*
São Jorge de Mina 69
São Tomé and Príncipe 70
savannah 3, 41
schools *See* education
science 43
sculpture 8, 48–50, *49*
Segu 43, 45
Senegal 119–120
Senegal River *41m*, 45, 100–102
Senkonyela 66
Shaka 62–64
sheep 24, 57, 97
shipbuilding 10, 68, 101
Shire River 109
Shona *56m*, 61, 119
Sidama 30
Sierra Leone 10, *41m*, 46, **86–87**, 101, 106, *124m*
silver 71, 76
Slave Coast 82–83
slave trade and slavery **76–88**; abolition of 22, 85–88, 95, 99, 100–103, 106, 108, 124–125; in agriculture 53, 70, 74, 76–78, 80, 85, 88, 91, 121; with Americas 70, 76–80, 85, 87–88; competition for 47, 71, 83; East Africa 29, 33–39, 75, 82, 88, 103, 117; with Europeans 10, 45, 46, 69–71, 75, 76–82, 81, 85, 88; impact of 54, 82–85, 88, 99; North Africa 9, 14, 18–21, 23, 77; precolonial 77; rebellions 117; southern Africa 91, 93; for warriors 8, 24, 37, 44; West Africa 42, 46–49, 51–54, 69–71, 77–78, 80, 82–88, 102, 106, 121
Sobhuza 62
Sofala *27m*, 39, 73
Sokoto *41m*, 43–45, 48, 121
Somali *27m*, 30, 103, 116
Songhai 8, *13m*, 23, *41m*, 42–43, 45
sorghum 51, 60
Sotho 10, *56m*, 60, 62, 65, 98
South Africa *See* Transvaal
southern Africa 6, **55–66**, **89–98**, **122–124** *See also name of country, culture*

Southern Rhodesia (Zimbabwe) 61, 118–119, *124m*
South-West Africa (Namibia) 119, 122, *124m*
Spain 20, 78, *124m*
Spanish Guinea *124m*
Spanish Sahara *124m*
Speke, John 109
spices 6, 39, 49, 69, 75, 89
Stanley, H. M. 38, 109–111, *110*
steamships 101, 103, 104
steppe 3
Sudan, the 8–9, 31, 40, 42–46, 109, 115, 120, *124m*
Suez Canal 19, 104, 114
sugar 18, 38, 70, 76, 80, 85, 87–88, 97
Susenyos 73
Swahili (language) 28, 39
Swahili city-states 9, 26–28, *27m*, 37–39, 58, 61, 68, 71–74, 77, 88, 117–118, 121
Swazi *56m*, 61, 63, 64
Swaziland 123, *124m*

Tanganyika 116
Tanzania 82
tariquas (religious brotherhoods) 21
taxes and tribute 18–19, 29, 33, 35–37, 39, 43, 46–47, 53, 60, 65, 69, 74, 83, 117–118
technology 10, 68, 78, 103, 112
Tewodros II 29–30, 103
textiles 14, 20, 33, 36, 47, 51, 53, 58, 68–70, 83, 125
Thembu 61
Timbuktu 23, 42, *43*, 108, 109
tin 31, 125
Tippu Tip (Hamed bin Muhammed) *27m*, **38**, *41m*, 121
Tlokwa (Batlokwa) *56m*, 66
tobacco 33, 36, 57, 59, 76, 80
Togo 119, *124m*
tortoiseshell 68
Torwa 10, 35–36
Toure, Samori 45–46
trade: East Africa 1, 9, 26, 31–39, 71–74, 102–103; European 67, 100–104, 111, 113, 116, 119, 121, 125; North Africa 1, 5–8, 12, 15–16, 18–24, 103, 116; Portuguese 1, 67–75; Sahara 1, 9, 12, 20, 24, 45; southern Africa 57–58, 61–62, 89, 92; triangular 80, 85; West Africa 41–46, 51–54, 69–71, 86–87, 100–102, 121; *See also* slaves
trade routes: ancient 6; caravans 14, 33, 37, 108; competition for 18, 34–35, 37, 100; control of 32, 34, 44; East Indies 103; to India 10–12, 18, 67–68, 74–75, 94–95, 103–104; oceans 26, 68, 89, 103; provisioning bases 59, 89–90; railroads 104; rivers and lakes 35, 101–103
trading companies 75, 79, 90–94, 113, 117–118, 121–122
Transvaal (South Africa) 97, 98, 122–123, *124m*

treaties 21, 65, 74, 94, 101, 111, 113, 116, 118, 120, 122
trekboers 92–96, *192*
triangular trade 80, 85
tribute *See* taxes and tribute
Tripoli *13m*, 19–21, 77, 114, *124m*
Tswana 10, *56m*, 60, 64
Tuareg 8, *13m*, 24–25, *41m*
Tukolor *41m*, 45, 82, 120
Tunis *13m*, 19–22, 77
Tunisia 114, *124m*
Turkey *See* Ottomans

Ubangi-Chari (Central African Republic) 120, *124m*
Uganda 117
'Umar, al-Hajj 45
United States 86–88, 106

vegetables 6, 60
veld 60, *61*, 66, 96–98
Victoria Falls 109
voortrekkers 96–97

Wahhabis 19
wars *See name of war*
weapons *See* firearms
weaving *See* textiles
Wesleyan Methodist Missionary Society 106
West Africa 6, **40–54**, *41m*, **69–71**, 100–102, **119–122** *See also name of country, culture*
wheat 91
wildlife 2–3
women: among nomads 24–25; in Islam 17; matrilineal inheritance 46; as rulers 66; as slaves 77, 81; as warriors 47, 63
wood 48, 50, 87
wool 36, 97
work permits 95
World and Africa, The (W. E. B. DuBois) 125

xenophobia 114
Xhosa 61–62, 82, 93–96, 122

Yao *27m*, 37, 117–118
Yoruba 8, *41m*, 45, 46–48, 69, 82, 121

Zaire River *See* Congo River
Zambezi River 2, *27m*, 35–37, 53, 66, 74, 109, 122
Zambia *See* Northern Rhodesia
Zanzibar *27m*, 39, 72, 88, 103, 109, 117
zawiyas (religious centers) 24
Zimbabwe *See* Southern Rhodesia
Zulu *56m*, **61–64**, 65, 66, 97, 122
Zuurveld 93
Zwide 62